/ oo

Barefoot in

MW00682623

BAREFOOT IN THE BOARDROOM

Venture and misadventure in the
People's Republic of China

Bill Purves

NC Press Limited

©Copyright Bill Purves, 1991

No part of this publication may be reproduced, stored in a
retrieval system, or transmitted, in any form or by any means,
electronic, mechanical, photocopying, recording or otherwise,
without the prior written permission of NC Press Limited.

First Published in 1991
Allen & Unwin Pty Ltd, Australia

Canadian Cataloguing in Publication Data

Purves, Bill
  Barefoot in the boardroom: venture and misadventure
  in the People's Republic of China

  ISBN 1-55021-079-3

  1. International business enterprises – China.
  2. Joint ventures – China. I. Title.

338.730951

We would like to thank the Ontario Arts Council and the Canada Council for
their assistance in the production of this book.
New Canada Publications, a division of NC Press Limited,
Box 452, Station A, Toronto, Ontario, Canada, M5W 1H8.

Set in 11/12.5 pt Bembo by Adtype Graphics, North Sydney

Printed and bound in Canada

For all those who endure

Contents

Foreword to the Canadian edition

Three years on, communism's spectacular collapse has had little impact on life at the Gold Land foundry. The workers are aware that their country is one of the last on "the socialist road" – China no longer tries to shield its citizens from developments of that magnitude – but ordinary citizens remain well trained not to form opinions on such matters. They still wait for opinions to be formed "at the centre" and transmitted to them for adherence.

The centre's latest opinion is that China should adopt elements of capitalism within Lenin's unreformed one-party state. The leaders are betting that steadily improving living conditions and social stability will be enough to forestall calls for political reform.

The story of *Barefoot in the Boardroom* suggests that they might get away with it. Certainly, Gold Land's managers and workers have had their difficulties in adapting to Western business practices. But the workers have now multiplied their incomes several times over. Families own their own television sets. School fees that used to be a burden now seem derisory. Three years on, it's working.

HongKong
April 1992

Preface

I never suspected it would be such an adventure. I was changing jobs and had been sending out résumés and scanning the classifieds for months. The ad was small and inconspicuous, but the words 'General Manager' caught my eye and I sent off a standard application letter without any particular enthusiasm. It seemed unlikely that I would stumble on a genuinely senior position in the classifieds, but in Hong Kong postage is cheap. And that was how it started.

It was early 1988, and I had been in Hong Kong about five years. Since the early 1980s, China's 'open door' economic policies and low labour costs had been attracting a growing tide of Hong Kong entrepreneurs who set up factories on the mainland to manufacture for the world market. I had never been involved in the China trade. In fact, I'd rarely visited the place. But I had worked hard to master the language and I understood a bit about the motivations of my Chinese colleagues in Hong Kong. So when I was offered the top job in a new joint-venture company to be set up in a small farming community in Western Guangdong Province, I jumped at the opportunity.

This is the story of my adventure. I wasn't attacked by bandits or laid low by malaria. But there were bandits aplenty, and diseases of the spirit. I know of a handful of Japanese, and two or three Westerners, who have lived the adventure of taking over and running an old-line Chinese work unit. There are surely

others—perhaps as many as a hundred in all—but none of them
have told the story. I'm going to try, because I hope that the
situation in China will continue to improve. I hope that in ten
years' time all of this will be ancient history and that life in
China will be much more like life in the West.

What I have to say is based on my personal observations and
impressions. China is a big place, and to the extent that I slip
into generalisations about China as a whole my generalisations
are inevitably wrong. You won't find any statistics here. China is
overrun with the ridiculously precise statistics of scientific socialism. They're wrong, too—not mistaken like my over-
enthusiastic generalisations, but systematically biased to earn a
bonus or prove a point. So I've left them all out.

Many writers about China admit that they were drawn to
their subject by an uninformed enthusiasm for Maoism, and that
this later turned to bitter disappointment and despair. My own
conversion has been rather the reverse. I have never been an
enthusiast or apologist for Communism or for China, so I
entered China with minimal expectations. My story may in part
seem critical, but during my stay I developed a profound respect
and sympathy for the Chinese people and all that they endure.

1

Office hours

IT's 6.45 a.m. on another workday morning at Gold Land
Limited, a cast iron foundry in rural China. Smoke from the
smouldering rubbish heaps mingles with the last of the morning
mist. Chickens forage in the courtyard. At the open drain outside the office block the General Manager is emptying his office
spittoon.

Gold Land Limited is a joint-venture company set up in 1988
to take advantage of new Chinese regulations encouraging joint
ventures between government-owned Chinese 'work units' and
foreign businesses. The factory itself has been here for decades,
but this joint venture is something new. There are only a few
thousand Chinese–foreign joint ventures operating in the whole
country, and only a handful with a Western General Manager.
At Gold Land that's me, the one emptying the spittoon.

Gold Land is in the town of Gaozhou at the western edge of
Guangdong Province, the province bordering Hong Kong.
Guangdong is at the leading edge of China's modernisation
efforts; and, as a joint venture, Gold Land is at the leading edge
of the leading edge. Our factory is not typical of factories in
Guangdong any more than Guangdong is typical of all China.
But there's a good chance that Gold Land today points the way
for the future of business and the Chinese worker in China as a
whole.

The working day officially begins at 7 o'clock, but the office

1

employees arrive early to spend ten or fifteen minutes cleaning the offices and a portion of the adjoining courtyard. The General Manager pitches in like everyone else in this daily ablution. First man in sweeps the floor with the broom kept behind the door. Someone else dusts down the desks with an old-fashioned duster made from chicken feathers. The ashtrays, the single wastebasket and the spittoon all need emptying. The last person to arrive washes out yesterday's teacups and puts out the vacuum flasks for refilling by the women who come around with the hand-pushed tank of boiled water. Someone turns over a new page on all the desk calendars, perhaps reading out the day's trivia tidbit. Once a week someone must remember to wind the clock. The office cleaning is completed by 7.15 and by 7.30 we have our first visitor.

Our foundry has 1000 employees, but the office staff occupy just nine small rooms. My office is much the same size as the others, but it feels more spacious as it houses fewer people. In one corner are two desks facing each other; these are for myself and my Assistant General Manager, Mr Go Gwong Hang. Mr Go doubles as our Manufacturing Manager, so he works late almost every evening, getting the daily shipments on the road. In the early morning he often goes for acupuncture treatment for a chronic sore shoulder, so he's rarely here at 7 o'clock.

In the opposite corner are desks for two members of our Board of Directors, Mr Chow Gai Chuen, Chairman of the Board, and Mr Chin Pui Lok, our Party Secretary. Until two years ago Mr Chow was the Factory Director of the Gaozhou Foundry, the traditional state-owned work unit that was merged into this new joint-venture company. He's one of only a few university graduates in all of Gaozhou county. As former Factory Director, he would be one of Gaozhou's most influential citizens even if his brother were not Vice-Mayor in charge of the local Public Security Bureau. Mr Chow has now given up control of the foundry to me as the General Manager of Gold Land, but his annual bonus from the state still depends on the economic performance of the joint venture. In effect, his bonus depends on my performance, and my strange Western management practices make Mr Chow very nervous.

Mr Chin is also an engineering graduate and, like Mr Chow,

has spent his whole working life in the foundry, but these days Mr Chin works primarily for the Communist Party. In the old foundry organisation his influence was equal to that of Mr Chow, leading the parallel chain of political command that permeates the foundry as it does every institution of Chinese society. Unlike Mr Chow, his control over the network of party cells has not been altered by the foundry's conversion to a joint venture. Indeed, he might say that since we're now on the frontier of encroaching capitalism, his role in overseeing the ideological health of the employees is more important than ever. But he'd say it in a nice way. Like successful politicos everywhere, Mr Chin comes across as a nice guy.

The décor might be considered somewhat depressing for an executive office. The walls, ceiling and floor are simply whitewashed cement which the ever-present foundry dust has made grey and dingy. Cobwebs hang in black tendrils from the ceiling. We take the broom to them occasionally, but the general ambiance discourages us from doing this as often as we should. Unfortunately, the lighting is not all it might be. Two naked bulbs hang on long cords from the ceiling. The desks are grouped in two blocks, and a bulb is pulled into position over the centre of each block by a string tied to the socket and running to a nail driven into the wall. The bulbs don't really give enough light, and they cast some nasty shadows, but then not much paperwork is done around here.

The office has two large windows: one in the front wall next to the door and another at the back. These windows are open day and night throughout the year, as we need the cross-ventilation. Although we are at ground level only 15 metres from the highway, the traffic is mostly bicycles so it's not particularly noisy. Keeping the windows open does, however, let in the dust and mosquitoes.

Apart from the two light bulbs, our office sports one other electrical appliance: a large, variable-speed ceiling fan which makes office work bearable during the hot summer months. Hidden within the four desks you could find three pocket calculators, but other than that our office is devoid of all the 'essential' office equipment. There are no typewriters, telephones, fax

3

machines or dictating equipment. And without all that paraphernalia what need have we of filing cabinets, or even paper and pens? Well, if you look around you could find some paper and pens, but where you would normally expect to find filing cabinets our office has a couch.

The corner near the door has a small table with two teapots, a dozen small teacups and three vacuum flasks of hot water. The remaining corner is taken up by the couch. Most of the work of the office centres around the couch and the tea table, as the principal activity of the General Manager's office consists of hosting a perpetual meeting.

The participants in this daily marathon are the normal visitors to any office: fellow employees who have come to discuss matters of company business. In fact, the General Manager's office at Gold Land has fewer of these visitors than is normal in a Chinese business, because Gold Land has installed a Western-style organisation structure with authority delegated to the various department heads. The foremen often visit with the intractable problems that beset foremen everywhere. Mrs Wong, the Quality Control Manager, comes in frequently with her particular concerns. And Ah Bo, the Purchasing Manager, has to deal with the serious problem of locating, buying and finding transport for our raw materials, so he visits more often than would normally be necessary in the West. On the other hand, we see relatively little of Mr Ho, the Accounting Manager. He has few of the sophisticated tools and techniques available to his Western counterpart, so we are unable to have many necessary discussions about cost control and pricing.

Whatever their purpose, all these visitors and many others wander in unannounced and with no thought of an appointment. They pour themselves a cup of tea, take a seat wherever one might be available and tune in to whatever business is going on. They do this in two ways that I at first found quite disconcerting. Everyone feels welcome to participate in any discussion. And, while they're waiting for an opening, everyone feels free to read whatever documents happen to be lying about. So a driver who has dropped in to ask about the schedule for a trip to town doesn't hesitate to participate in a discussion of pricing policy

4

initiated by the Sales or Accounting Manager. He's weak on the technicalities, of course, but like everyone else he has worked in the factory all his life and will do so until he retires, so he has a good basic grasp of factory affairs and a vital stake in the firm's success.

There are normally half a dozen people in the office at any one time. A new arrival with something on his mind has the choice of settling down to await a break in the discussion, or of interrupting loudly in hope of diverting the attention of the General Manager away from the topic at hand and on to the one he has come to discuss. Most visitors choose the latter approach, loudly broaching their new subject while still a step or two outside the doorway. This is often successful, but by the same token the success is often short-lived, as the next arrival invokes the same ploy. From the General Manager's point of view the office is often full of half-finished discussions opened like the layers of an onion. Each of the half-dozen occupants of the office is in the middle of a suspended discussion on some point of interest to himself, and meanwhile participating in the suspended and active discussions of later arrivals.

To supplement their cups of tea these pending interlocutors pass around the last vital element of our office equipment: the bamboo water-pipe. Most Chinese men, and in private many Chinese women, are heavy smokers. Even this élite, the employees of a foreign joint venture, can't afford to smoke cigarettes. The alternative is the cheap, locally grown tobacco, which is unblended and badly cured. It makes for rough smoking when rolled, but is bearable when filtered through water or tea in the water-pipe.

These pipes are a feature of most public and private facilities in this part of China. Even the public buses provide them for the diversion of passengers. The bowl of the pipe is just large enough to hold one small pinch of tobacco at a time, so the smoker gets only one or two deep puffs before the tobacco is consumed. He savours it while rolling another ball to continue the process. It's a lot of work, and it burns up a lot of matches, but one result is that the amount of tobacco consumed is limited—especially as there is normally someone else waiting for a turn. In our office the tobacco and matches are supplied, but when calling for the pipe in a restaurant or other public facility the user is expected to supply his own. He's also expected to ignore the hundreds of strangers who have pulled at the same mouthpiece before him.

A major part of upgrading the management of the foundry has involved supplementing these friendly confabs with a bit of paperwork. The paperwork burden around Gold Land is still refreshingly light by Western standards, but at least our dealings with outside parties are now documented by purchase orders, sales confirmations and invoices. Previously, as is typical of many Chinese enterprises, most of this work was done verbally.

When I first introduced these paperwork systems, I ran into some unexpected problems. During my first day on the job I discovered, for example, that my desk was not of much use. In the first place, it's very small, as wood is scarce and expensive in China. And it has no file drawer. Indeed, there are no file drawers, or even file folders, in the whole company. A collection of papers on a particular subject is rather rare, but when the need arises (as with a set of monthly production schedules or financial reports), the papers are usually clipped to a clipboard and hung from a nail driven into the wall. I began keeping my files in large manila envelopes and stacking them in a bookcase, but it's awkward to retrieve envelopes from the bottom of a pile.

My desk has several normal drawers, and I wondered initially how I should use these if there were no documents to store. Seeking guidance, I checked the desks of some of my colleagues. They were full of a strange collection of things: insecticide spray, running shoes, folding umbrellas, newspapers, towels, tea and various items of clothing. Some also had a calculator. They were not (including the calculator) things these people would use every day. Which explains why they weren't troubled by the fact that the drawers are so difficult to open.

This access problem isn't the fault of the desk. It's well constructed, and the drawers run smoothly enough. It's a status problem. The fancy executive chairs of a Western office are unavailable in China, and would in any case be unbearably hot and sweaty in the summer heat. Instead, the last word in executive status is a high-backed armchair, hand-woven in rattan. It's

6

cool, easy to clean and attractive by any standard. It's also comfortable to sit in. But it doesn't fit under the desk, and the full,
sweeping arms block the drawers. To open a drawer you must
first half-rise and hitch the chair to one side so that the arms are
out of the way. Well, I suppose if you're reaching for your
umbrella or running shoes you were planning to get up anyway.

The next problem with systematising the paperwork was to
purchase some paper. On my first day at Gold Land, finding no
paper in my new desk, I innocently set out to acquire some.
There are no secretaries, so this involved a personal visit to the
Administration Department. They were most anxious to help
the new Western General Manager, but my request for paper was
a rather unusual one. They rummaged around and eventually
proposed three possibilities. The factory had some onion-skin,
airmail-style paper printed with the letterhead of the old
foundry. This was used for sending the odd official letter. For
written communication within the foundry they had a small
notepaper-size version of the same thing. Finally, they had some
sheets of rough newsprint used to mimeograph official
announcements to be distributed in multiple copies. None of
these possibilities conformed to A4 or any other standard dimen-
sion. The newsprint wasn't even the shape of a normal written
page.

I took away some of the letter and notepaper and soon got
used to using it. It works well enough if you keep your communications to one page and don't try to erase anything. Reading a
two-page document involves pulling the two pages apart so that
you don't see the second page through the first. But working in
the Western way I quickly wrote enough reports, notes and
memos to use up the entire supply. In replenishing it I asked the
administration staff to try to find some conventional, opaque, A4
lined pads. Two years later, they're still looking. On trips to
Hong Kong I always bring back a few lined pads and they
disappear quickly. The closest equivalent available in China
would be the exercise books used by schoolchildren.

It's not that Chinese businesses demand this onion-skin paper
because they send a lot of airmail letters. Far from it. Although
China is as large as Canada, all domestic mail travels by train and

truck. The point of onion-skin paper is that it facilitates making carbon copies. In the absence of xerography (a sensitive technology in any totalitarian state), carbon paper lives on in China as a cost-effective, low-tech substitute. It's widely available, and the quality is pretty serviceable. I had never had much experience with the stuff, but it quickly teaches you to write carefully and avoid mistakes. There's no white liquid to cover errors, and it's a chore to erase the copies with cheap Chinese erasers. The Chinese favour a double-sided carbon paper, so each paper in the stack comes away printed front and back. My colleagues pointed out that anyone who tries to alter his copy of a contract must alter both the front and back sides, and he knows that whoever holds the copies above and below his has original imprints of what he has altered. Apparently the police sometimes use this feature in investigating allegations of fraud.

Over the course of a couple of years I've pursued my own private programme of technology transfer. It began with a plastic pen box. I brought one back from a visit to Hong Kong, along with a couple of boxes of pencils and a handful of cheap pens. You can buy pens and pencils in China, but the pens don't write very well and the pencils don't last long. The leads are often broken inside, and the rubber breaks off the first time you try to erase something. So my imported pens and pencils and my new pen box were a big hit. Paper clips, staplers, adhesive tape and rubber bands made a similar impression. These small items set us apart from the other industries in the area where glue, pins and string comprise the main items of office equipment. But the real blockbuster was white correcting fluid. There had never been a good way to erase erroneous characters on the flimsy Chinese paper. Any serious erasure quickly put a hole right through. The characters of written Chinese are complicated, and a small mistake in one part of a character would often require crossing out the whole thing and starting again. After a few such mistakes the whole page looks so messy that it must be rewritten. The little white bottle with its little white brush not only produced neater documents, but the Chinese also enjoyed practising their calligraphy with this new and unwieldy instrument. I couldn't smuggle the stuff in fast enough.

My arrival at Gold Land helped to drive a small nail in the

coffin of traditional brushwork. Before I arrived, the common alternative to the brush in business correspondence was the fountain-pen. The two or three people who wrote letters and reports for external consumption each had a collection of three or four fountain-pens with different nibs suitable for writing characters of various sizes on different grades of paper. When I innocently dumped from my briefcase a variety of felt-tipped marking pens, varying from very fine points up to bold highlighters, they caused a sensation.

The lack of modern office equipment leaves managers in a Chinese factory with fewer management techniques at their disposal. To a large extent managers have to rely on just walking round to gather, analyse and use information. Gold Land has only about 25 managers. Most are in their thirties, which means they were in their teens during the Cultural Revolution when for several years schools were at a standstill and for about ten years in turmoil. So our managers didn't receive the best possible basic education and their subsequent work experience has done nothing to strengthen their basic skills. Calculations other than additions and subtractions are awkward to do on an abacus, and written reports are difficult to use effectively without a filing system. All copies must be made with carbon paper, then filed in manila envelopes on bookshelves. The whole process is so clumsy that it's simply not used, so the managers have forgotten many of the reading, writing and calculating skills they once knew. They are left with only two management mechanisms: the open meeting, and management by walking around. Mr Go, as the Manufacturing Manager, tends to spend much of his day walking around, with a few periods of marathon open discussion. In my case the balance is tipped the other way. I spend most of the day receiving visitors and must extricate myself to put in visits to the various operating departments.

With no telephone and no formal meetings in the Western sense, multi-focused discussion is the essence of office routine in the Chinese factory. Tea is continually on offer, so there are no coffee breaks, and the entire morning often passes with no other activity. Fortunately, it sometimes becomes necessary to consult someone not immediately present. Since there is no way to do so over the phone, this provides a welcome opportunity to wander

9

down and join the discussion in progress in one of the other offices. First, though, it's necessary to close all of the interrupted discussions pending on the lips of the various visitors. This done, one becomes the aggressor, barging into a web of deliberations-in-progress hosted by someone else.

There is one major variation in this routine, which is played out two or three times a week. It's initiated by that other class of callers to a Chinese office: the delegation. A delegation is a group of visitors (they always travel in groups, never singly) from outside the circle of factory employees who have come to sell something, to buy something or, most often, to 'study our situation'. Since in most factories the Factory Director is the Emperor figure who makes all the decisions, the sellers and buyers begin their visit by calling on the Factory Director. In our factory they assume initially that they should begin with me, but after some social chat I try to pass them on quickly to the appropriate line manager. The study tours will insist on speaking to the Factory Director and no one else, presumably because in most factories no one else is allowed to say anything of consequence.

Delegations break up the office routine because they are received not in the office, but in the meeting room. The Chinese name for this is the 'Meeting Guests Room', which is in fact all it's ever used for. As in Western business, these delegations have a pecking order. But I find the Chinese pecking order quite inscrutable, so I classify them as either announced or unannounced. Chinese business etiquette does not require guests to have an appointment. Indeed, with no telephones, making appointments would be quite a problem. Be that as it may, these visitors are the ultimate conversation bargers.

A delegation normally arrives by truck. Our first warning of the unannounced variety is when a strange vehicle pulls into the courtyard. Mr So, our Administration Manager, is a long-time resident, employee and party member who is adept at sizing up the status of delegations at a glance. He has the job of alerting the woman who maintains the Meeting Guests Room and choosing the standard of hospitality to be offered. Tea, of course, is *de rigeur*. But more important visitors rate fruit, cigarettes and, at the highest levels, soft drinks.

As the General Manager, my first task is to wind up whatever discussions are in progress and get out into the courtyard to shake hands. Were they to enter the office, the visitors would, like everyone else, feel free to pick up and read whatever documents happened to be lying around. If the delegation has somehow warned us of their arrival, the Meeting Guests Room will be in readiness and I can lead them to it immediately. Unannounced visitors must be delayed in the courtyard with a few minutes of small talk. This can present some problems, as I often have no idea at all who it is that I'm greeting and why they might have chosen to come.

Entertaining visitors involves meeting in a different room and discussing more general topics, but it's a meeting just the same. For a Westerner, this rhythm and style of office life takes some getting used to. There's no in-tray to organise your day. The endless day-long discussions shift from topic to topic as new participants enter, so it's hard to keep track of what has been decided. When a decision is reached there's no easy way to disseminate it until the next weekly management meeting. And on rainy days you have to get used to chickens running around under the desks and, when he has a cold, a manager blowing his nose on the floor.

I chose at the outset to leave these quaint office customs alone and to focus instead on a few essentials: quality, on-time delivery and cost control. In time, I was able to prove to myself that by working through Gold Land's strange office culture we could nevertheless deliver progress in these key areas.

I eventually came to enjoy these disorganised days in the office. The day-long give and take becomes a comfortable way to exchange information and to motivate the other managers. And there is another attractive feature of our office life. Quitting time is 5.00 p.m., and it's a rare evening that we put in any overtime. Because 5 o'clock is also supper time, and by 5.30 the canteen runs out of food.

2

A guided tour

U NTIL 1988 Gold Land was known as the Gaozhou Foundry. It had been started about 30 years earlier as an offshoot of the Gaozhou Number One Foundry to specialise in making cast iron agricultural equipment. We still make some agricultural equipment, but over the past ten years the foundry has been doing more and more export business with a firm of manufacturers' representatives in Hong Kong called Landmann Limited.

Gold Land is a joint venture between these two long-standing business partners, and the name is formed by combining the first Chinese characters of the names of the two firms. The English pronunciation of the two characters would be 'Go Long' but as we're not a hard-sell stock brokerage 'Gold Land' was considered both easy to pronounce and suitably optimistic. The Chinese put much emphasis on naming and will often change their personal names to reflect their changing situations in life. My Chinese name, for example, is Pak Wai Si; but when I lived in Hong Kong I did a lot of competitive running under the name San Hang Tai Bo, a famous character from Chinese legend who was able to walk 500 miles in a day and 100 miles in a night. The Chinese, coming from that cultural tradition, consider our strange name a success. Though Gold Land has yet to stumble across the mother lode.

In fact, it may be some time before we hit pay-dirt, as our business is cast iron. Our biggest lines are barbecue grilles, fireplace andirons, park benches and various other items that could be collectively described as 'recreational housewares'. It's an unglamorous, low-tech business that amounts to making pre-shaped holes in the sand, pouring in molten iron, then grinding down and painting the resulting cast lump. It's heavy, dirty work and insufferably hot in the summer.

We're relatively successful at it, thanks primarily to our staff, who have survived a lifetime of state socialism, with the Cultural Revolution thrown in for good measure. After that, labouring in a tropical foundry appears a pretty attractive proposition. And why not? The alternative is tilling a rice paddy up to the knees in muck under a blazing sun. In other countries it's difficult to recruit employees for cast iron foundries, but in Gaozhou it's still the best work available.

Ours is the largest foundry in Guangdong Province, but as you wend your way through the stream of pedestrians, bicycles, ox-carts and garden tractors on the highway entering Gaozhou from the south, you're as likely as not to miss it entirely. Like all Chinese factories, Gold Land is surrounded by a 4-metre-high brick wall topped with broken glass. The sole gate is marked on the highway by a modest sign in Chinese characters and two official nameplates on the gate posts. The gate is guarded 24 hours a day and is opened only to admit vehicles.

I scoffed at all this security until the day our office meeting was interrupted by the arrival of a young cowherd. He'd come, he explained, to claim a reward. It seems that a few weeks previously this youngster had been tending his cows in the fields behind the factory when he noticed one of our employees lowering a piece of equipment over the wall on a rope. He'd reported it to the guards, but they had been slow in paying the conventional reward. It was the first I'd heard of it, but enquiries revealed that the culprit would be appearing in court in a few days' time. (The reward was payable only on conviction, though in Chinese law any case that's brought to court presumes the guilt of the accused. To acquit him would cause the Public Security Bureau to lose face.) It appeared that some former employees of another foundry had decided to set up a private casting business, but had no way to get an equipment allocation from the state. This kind of equipment is not available on the free market, so they thought they might get started by stealing some from us!

The factory stretches for 100 metres along the highway and reaches back 800 metres into the surrounding paddy fields. In most respects it resembles a medieval walled town more than a factory. About 800 people live within the walls. The factory has its own clinic, library, day-care centre, bicycle repairman, barber and branch bank. There's a small meat and vegetable market, a park, and every bit of unused space is taken up by the employees' small vegetable plots.

But all of this is not evident at once. Instead, on entering the gate, the first impression is of a large cement courtyard occupied, at most times of day, only by a few foraging turkeys. This large open area serves as the public square of Gold Land, where children play, retired workers take the sun in winter and couples stroll in the evening. Once or twice a day a motor vehicle (a truck, only rarely a car) comes to Gold Land, and then the square serves temporarily as our parking lot.

The plaza is bounded on three sides by three-storey cement buildings. A stretch of the ground floor is given over to offices, but all the rest is employees' housing. The buildings are the same drab, badly painted affairs seen everywhere in China. Each storey is partitioned into a long row of 3- by 4-metre boxes, each with a door and window in the front and a single window at the back. A long external balcony runs the length of the building on each floor. From the plaza it looks like a run-down motel, but the interiors rather bring a prison to mind.

As in a medieval town, the people living around the plaza have no inside plumbing, so they have a habit of throwing waste water off their balconies without warning. In fact, these housing units really have no facilities at all except a naked light bulb hanging from the ceiling and an electric outlet on the wall. The windows are barred so they can be kept open all summer to maximise ventilation. Most employees use their one electric plug to run a fan. But then there is little other choice, as the wiring won't support anything more powerful. Each of these residential units houses from two to as many as eight people.

Along the fourth side of the plaza is a row of four garages. In China, motor vehicles are still relatively rare. Cars are particularly scarce, and private cars are virtually unknown. In fact, it's only in recent years that cars have ceased to turn heads in Gaozhou. The first cars in this area were taxis chartered to bring visitors from distant cities, so around Gaozhou the term for a car in Cantonese is 'taxi-car'. And Gaozhou, it should be remembered, is in China's most prosperous province.

As befits the status of a foreign joint-venture company, Gold Land boasts a number of impressive vehicles. Like most factories, we have an ageing Chinese-made Liberation 5-ton truck and a Beijing-made Jeep. But in addition Gold Land can boast a $1\frac{1}{2}$-ton Toyota pickup, a new Toyota 4-door sedan and an ageing Toyota van. These are known in Cantonese as the farming truck, the taxi-car and the loaf-of-bread car, respectively. (They eat no bread in these parts, but the van is white and resembles what people imagine a loaf of bread to look like.) Each vehicle has a permanent driver who tends it jealously. Every night the vehicles are locked away in the garages, but during the day they are often left on display in the plaza for the inspiration of visitors. Away from the factory they are never left parked on the street. Parts, after all, are hard to get.

From the front gate, along one side of the plaza, a long straight road leads back through the centre of the factory. On the left an unbroken wall of badly painted cement buildings fronts directly on to the road. But along the front wall of these buildings is a row of bedraggled but defiant leafy bushes, each about a metre high. On the right-hand side the buildings sit back 5 to 10 metres from the road, and this setback is fenced off by similar bushes into a series of small lawns, each sporting one or two trees. The trees—legacies of past beautification campaigns—are of various types. Most are now fully mature, and they lend a bit of relief to what would otherwise be a less-than-inspiring streetscape.

The clay soil of Gaozhou makes excellent adobe, and around the Gaozhou area there are still many buildings of mud brick. In recent years, relative prosperity has led to the rebuilding of many of these adobe structures with properly fired bricks. Brick and

15

cement kilns are numerous in this area, and these days conventional brick construction is the method of choice. Our factory has now replaced all of its adobe buildings with structures of reinforced concrete. The architecture of all these new buildings is almost identical, for a rather special reason.

One of the new joint venture's first investments was to build a new packing and shipping workshop. Mr Chow was in charge of getting the necessary permissions, and one day he showed up in the office with a roll of blueprints. 'I've got the inspector's approval,' he announced. 'Ask Old Chin to make an appointment at the bank tomorrow or the next day.' 'Well, that's nice,' I said. 'Can I have a look?' Mr Chow seemed a bit surprised that I should be so interested, but he unrolled the plans on the desk. I soon realised why he was surprised. These same plans had been used for every building the foundry had constructed over the past several years. They were the plans for a casting workshop. 'Mr Chow, this building doesn't seem to have a loading dock.' Now he was not only surprised, but getting apprehensive as well. 'No.' 'And the single storey has a 25-foot ceiling. We can't stack product 25 feet high. What will we do with all that head room?' I'd spoiled Mr Chow's day and uncovered another of the never-ending problems of cross-cultural communication.

As in many countries, a Chinese factory seeking to construct a new workshop must first apply for a building permit. The permit is granted based on a study of the plans. But architects competent to draw up acceptable plans are in short supply in rural China. The result is that at some time in the past the factory acquired a set of construction drawings for a foundry workshop building, and these same drawings are now resubmitted whenever a new building is required. It doesn't matter if the proposed building is to be a foundry, a machine shop or a warehouse. We have only one set of plans, and that's the building which is constructed. Apart from the waste, the result is an architectural monotony that is typical not just of our factory but of any Chinese town and most Chinese cities.

The central road through Gold Land passes a row of identical casting workshops which would not look out of place in a foundry anywhere in the world. As we'll see shortly, the scenes inside are literally infernal.

The road forks; one branch leads off to the left to the yards where we store our pig iron and coke, while the other leads into the heart of 'Gold Land Town', our accommodation area. In between is a walled park a few hundred square metres in area. Such parks are found in any sizeable Chinese factory. Ours is graced with various flowering plants, rock gardens, banana trees and a rather elaborate rock fountain. No one seems to use the park much, but in the summer young boys sometimes go skinny-dipping in the fountain. Just behind the park, arranged around a fish pond, are the buildings that form the centre of social life in Gold Land Town. The most important of these is the dining hall.

The majority of our employees are young men and women, single or living apart from their spouses. Some have been assigned by the state to work in this factory for life, but the majority are working on multi-year contracts. The state permanent workers normally live with their families in single rooms of 12 square metres, while the contract employees usually live in dormitory-style accommodation.

One day in early spring, Mr Ho our union leader, came to me with a request for some iron bunk beds. As often happens, I immediately set off on the wrong tack. 'Beds? We're not hiring any new employees. If anything, we're trying to reduce the workforce. What do we need more beds for?' 'The hot weather is coming,' he replied inscrutably. 'Hot weather—what does hot weather have to do with it?' 'Oh, General Manager, have a heart. People can sleep two to a bed in the winter time, but when the hot weather comes it's really too much to ask.'

A convincing argument. I had never suspected. We bought the beds, though we didn't really have adequate space for them.

None of the staff have facilities for cooking their own meals. Permanent and contract employees alike must eat 21 meals a week from the company dining hall. However, a few of the ground-floor accommodation units come with a small outside cooking shed. This offers the possibility of planning your own menu or rustling up a snack between meals, but only families with at least two members working full time in the factory can hope to be assigned one of these units. And then securing fire-wood or other fuel becomes a serious problem. So most residents of Gold Land Town make three trips each day to the dining hall.

The dining hall is an exception to the Gold Land architectural tradition, as it was built in rather special circumstances. The hall is a relic of the days of Chairman Mao and was the scene of the kangaroo courts of the Cultural Revolution. At one end is a stage, the proscenium arch still bearing the traces of revolutionary slogans. Hundreds of people sat on the cement floor and listened to the reading of the latest directive from the Central Committee. Set in the wall at the far end, opposite the stage, are two small barred windows. They might be ticket booths, except that no one needed tickets for the entertainments staged in this building. Instead, they open into a kitchen shed that has been tacked on to the outside of the building. These two small windows make this our dining hall.

Along the wall are racks holding the employees' meal cards. An employee takes down his card and presents it at the window when ordering his food. A blackboard above the windows presents the three choices for the current meal. There is always a vegetable dish, a dish with meat and vegetables, and a third which could also be described as meat and vegetable but it's made with the bones, fat and sinews and is less expensive than the second selection. In terms of US dollars, the prices of the three offerings range from about 5 cents for a helping of the vegetable dish to about 12 cents for the most expensive selection. At those prices the fare is less than exciting. Each diner brings his own metal bowl (really a small wash basin) and his own chopsticks. He pushes his meal card and bowl under the bars and states his selection. The server fills the basin with about half a cubic foot of rice and then upends a saucerful of the selected dish on top. The lucky gourmet then retires to his room, his workplace or any convenient site, to squat and eat. It's a system which in any Western prison would quickly cause a riot and probably lead to charges of maltreatment.

The labour regulations call for work units to provide each worker with 10 square metres of living space. This space is allocated for the use of the worker's entire family. There is a government-mandated minimum age for marriage in China. Although it varies from one part of the country to another, it's in

18

the early to mid-twenties. Almost every worker under the minimum age is single. On passing the minimum, most people quickly marry, and one year later the couple will have one child. Parents and child then become a new nucleus in the extended family system which connects them in a carefully ordered hierarchy of in-laws, cousins, uncles and so on. All the members of this extended family normally live in the surrounding area, as geographic mobility in China is very low. So, as the fortunes of various branches of the extended family wax and wane, the working couple will be expected from time to time to accommodate various ageing relatives and n'er-do-well cousins, or to foster a series of young children. All of this has no impact on their housing allocation. They must make do with their assigned 10 square metres.

Another important consideration is that there is no requirement that the 10 square metres comprise an entire room or a self-contained unit. It might be one room in a suite of rooms, half of a 20-square-metre room or 10 square metres in an enormous dormitory. There is no statutory provision for privacy but young singles find this rather enjoyable. At Gold Land, for example, we try to place all the young, unmarried members of our men's and women's basketball teams in adjoining units looking out on the basketball court. They are all within a few years in age and are all interested in basketball, popular music, and in having a good time, so it's a bit like a college dorm. When one of them marries we try to give the couple more family-oriented accommodation, but in principle the new couple could find themselves sharing with what in rural China passes for swinging singles.

A third important point is that the government housing standards apply only to workers. 'Worker' is a rather special term in China and, indeed, in Marxist theory. The housing standards, as well as all the other labour regulations, in principle apply only to individuals who are officially registered as members of the worker class, who have then been officially assigned to Gold Land's joint-venture partner, the Gaozhou Foundry, by the Labour Registration Bureau and who are thus members of our labour union. Strictly speaking, this describes about one-quarter of our 1000 employees. The others are a mixture of temporary, casual and contract employees who are not officially members of the worker class and therefore not within the ambit of the housing standards and the other labour regulations. Gold Land treats real workers and contract employees alike in housing matters, but this is purely a matter of company policy. In China as a whole, this equal treatment is highly unusual—by all accounts, unheard of.

The situation often arises where both husband and wife work in the factory. If they are both members of the worker class and are officially assigned to us, this should entitle them to 20 square metres of accommodation. If a husband and wife, both workers, are assigned to two different work units in the same town, they should receive 10 square metres at each work unit. A third situation is where one partner is a worker and the other a peasant. In this family the peasant doesn't count as far as the regulations are concerned. The worker continues to get his 10 square metres, but he may or may not be able to use it to accommodate his spouse. This explains why so many Chinese couples live apart through much of their marriage. Either, as two workers, they have been assigned to different work units too far apart for daily or even weekly commuting (no one, of course, has a private car), or the worker has been assigned to an urban area where the peasant spouse is not permitted to live. The Chinese have imposed strict residence controls to limit the migration that has led, in many developing countries, to vast shanty towns on the outskirts of the cities. China has no shanty towns, but family separations are common in those areas where the housing regulations are strictly applied.

Gold Land tries to alleviate the problems as best it can, but like every work unit we have too much labour, too many retired workers (and their families) and not enough accommodation. As a start, our standard housing unit is 12 square metres. Using this oversized unit, we try to give families the complete use of one unit; but on the other hand we ask singles, sometimes as many as four singles, to share. When husband and wife both work in the factory we can't hope to allocate two of these units to them, so we offer a slightly different advantage in the form of the ground-floor units which face a small shed across a walkway. Most people use this shed as a cookhouse to liberate themselves from our canteen menu, but one family converted theirs to a barber shop to earn some extra money after hours.

In the end there is still not enough housing to go around, so we bend the regulations to make a special deal with people who have access to housing outside the factory. An example might be a wife whose husband qualifies for better accommodation at his work unit than we can offer to her. Another common case is someone who has a house in a nearby village. (He doesn't own it, but the village recognises it as his family's house.) Under the regulations these people should have another 10 square metres of accommodation from us, but since we can't provide it we give them a monthly cash payment instead.

In most cases this is fair enough, but the payment also goes to a few senior managers who have managed to lease land and build private houses in town. In the Chinese situation it's fair to presume that this conspicuous wealth was acquired through various gifts and payments which in other countries would be considered gross improprieties, if not out-and-out felonies. It's a shame to be paying these few individuals to enjoy their ill-gotten private homes, but as long as their hands are no longer in the till there's not much we can do. They are entitled, like every worker, to their 10 square metres, and we cannot provide it.

There's little scope for originality in decorating a 3- by 4-metre box. The accommodation units are strung together in townhouse or motel style and are of brick with a cement or tile roof. The brick walls have been plastered over and whitewashed, and the view from inside includes a lot of plaster, as the row-house arrangement means that the two side walls are necessarily blank. The back wall has a window in the centre, and the front wall has a door in one corner and another window for cross-ventilation. As designed, the top-floor rooms have what could grandly be called a cathedral ceiling. In other words, the underside of the roofing tiles is exposed right up to the ridgepole.

The more expensive way to decorate such a space is to build in rafters and a level ceiling. This provides storage space under the roof, and a large-diameter, slow-speed tropical ceiling fan can then be installed to cool the room without bringing down the hot air from under the roof tiles. Those with less money or ambition leave the ceiling open and take up the limited space available with table fans.

The need for cross-ventilation dictates that the beds should line the two blank side walls. This leaves room for a wardrobe or two, a small table under the back window between the beds and a sideboard along the front wall under the window. A radio, perhaps a television, and that's it. There are no children's toys, no pets and, of course, no private toilet or cooking facilities.

The occupants normally expect to live in the same unit for years, even decades. As a result, you might expect some initiative in interior decorating, but in my experience this is very rare. My first inclination would be to buy some paint and inject some individuality, but individuality is not normally well regarded in Chinese society; and in any case, both paint and brushes are expensive. If the factory used a lot of paint, perhaps some would be diverted to decoration. But in a cast iron foundry almost every product is painted one or another shade of black. So I have never seen a repainted housing unit.

Screening the windows against the mosquitoes would be another obvious improvement. Rice paddies surround us just outside the walls, so we have no shortage of mosquitoes. Unfortunately, window screen is almost unobtainable. When I first moved to Gold Land I asked for my room to be screened and the maintenance staff managed to do it, but this was most unusual. A resident who managed to procure screening for his windows would then have to install a screen door. There are no such doors for sale, so anyone with the idea of screening his unit is faced with the daunting prospect of building a screen door from scratch. The maintenance staff managed to do this for me, but just getting suitable straight lumber was difficult. The result is that I live in the only screened housing unit at Gold Land.

The alternative to screening the windows is to install mosquito nets over the beds. Mosquito nets are readily available, but they certainly make a mess of the room. The most common sort is the square box used for bunk beds or a normal bed converted to a four-poster. Alternatively, you can buy an umbrella-shaped affair which hangs from a single central point. Some people find these claustrophobic, but they can be tied up during the day to hang in a big knot, leaving the bed clear for sitting, eating, reading and playing cards. With space at a premium this has some advantages.

Lighting in the housing units is limited, like so much else, by our difficulties in electricity supply. Guangdong Province has attracted a large share of the new investments during China's recent opening to the West. Guangdong's Pearl River delta has become, by most measures, China's most prosperous region and therefore its largest consumer of electricity. Gaozhou is not in the delta. Gaozhou county is situated in the foothills on the delta's western edge. All of the rivers, lakes and streams in the county have been controlled with dams and barrages equipped with small, primitive and inefficient hydroelectric generators. Since industrial development in the county is limited, these generators produce enough power to make the county a net exporter of electric power to the national grid. Sadly, electricity is not like coal or grain. Exporter status doesn't guarantee that there will be enough for consumption at home. A grid is a grid, and when demand exceeds supply, everyone connected to the grid must reduce his consumption to help keep the voltage up. So Gaozhou suffers, along with the delta, the growing pains of electric power shortages.

From the individual factory or the individual employee's point of view, the argument is not about cuts, but about how the cuts will be shared out. There are two broad strategies: brownouts, where everyone's voltage is lowered, or complete blackouts which rotate around through various parts of the system. No prizes for guessing that in China, with its clear-cut class system, the rotating-cuts method is favoured.

China is a planned economy, and allocation of power cuts is one aspect of the plan. Agriculture, for example, is a development priority. This doesn't protect the electricity supply to the small farming villages, but it guarantees that the fertiliser factory in Gaozhou has no power-cut problems. This is a defensible arrangement, perhaps, but what about the sugar refinery? It refines sugar only during the winter cane harvest but has the same year-round priority.

On sticky evenings when the power is off at Gold Land I used to sit and swelter on the roof of the office. Then one morning Mr Go asked why I never took refuge in the roadside shack across the highway where they serve tea and simple meals. He explained that some of the managers often spend their evenings there, as the fans always work. They can offer this advantage because they tap their electricity over the wall of the sugar refinery. It proved to be good advice.

As a foreign-backed joint venture, Gold Land doesn't enjoy the state-owned refinery's priority for electricity, so we are left to battle it out at the local level. Like many similar battles in China, winning tactics involve 'developing a good relationship' with the allocators—in this case, the Electricity Supply Bureau. This 'developing' normally takes the form of distributing television sets and refrigerators to the key decision makers, but at Gold Land we tried to avoid this crude approach and offered instead to help them import some foreign equipment.

This may not sound like much of an inducement until you consider that these government bureaux are measured not on their profitability or operating efficiency, but on investment and employment. And in the short term this importing process was structured in such a way that the heads of the Electricity Bureau qualified for a quasi-business trip to Hong Kong. This was the first, and perhaps the only, foreign trip of their lives, and in the context of the trip they might legally import their own television set, refrigerator, or even a motorcycle, without any clearly tainted cash passing through the hands or books of Gold Land. The resulting relationship is good, but by no means good enough to exempt us from power cuts. At best, we can perhaps suggest what hours would be least inconvenient.

Having done what we can to maintain our electricity supply, we have our own rationing problem within the factory. Casting iron is an energy-intensive business, but most of the energy comes from coke burned in the furnaces. Accordingly, the Gaozhou Foundry used to have various priorities in the government's allocation of coke, but not for investment in electrical equipment. The entire factory, with 1000 employees and 800 permanent residents, was supplied through a single ageing transformer rated at 460 kilowatts. It's unlikely that this was ever sufficient, even in the distant past when it was installed. But at the founding of the joint venture we calculated that the existing demand, before installing any new equipment, was already 1000 kilowatts, or more than twice the capacity.

Until we are able to install new transformers, rationing is enforced by methods rather like those of the Electricity Bureau. The power grid within the factory is divided into sub-grids. The first priority grid, at high voltage, powers the cranes, lathes and other heavy equipment. Next are the lights and miscellaneous power to the production areas. The last priority grid supports the accommodation areas: Gold Land Town.

On a typical summer's day the power is cut off completely in Gold Land Town throughout the day. Forget about owning a refrigerator. In the workshops, all the fans are going but the lights are off. At night, no one would be able to sleep inside their mosquito nets without a fan to force a bit of air circulation. So the power is on in Gold Land Town and the workshops can work on a limited basis, if at all. The changeover in the evening could cause problems, with plenty of arguments and special pleading, but in fact it doesn't, because evening is the time of peak demand all over Gaozhou county. In the evening Gold Land is often cut off completely until 10 or 11 o'clock.

If it's not hot enough to drive me to the roadside shack, I usually spend my evenings sitting on the roof watching for shooting stars or satellites. (There are no aeroplanes to confuse things around Gaozhou.) Most factory residents take a bath.

The Chinese must learn from infancy to distinguish between the water in streams and rivers (for agriculture), water from the tap (for washing) and water from the vacuum flask—the only kind you can drink. Any infant who failed to learn this basic lesson has probably long since succumbed to some horrible disease.

The rivers and streams of China are terribly polluted. They look muddy, they smell of sewage, and even wading across one raises images of every sort of skin disease and worm infestation. On the other hand, there are no plastic bags snagged in the shallows and no discarded refrigerators or car bodies rusting on the banks. In wading across you'll never cut your foot on a broken bottle. The pollution comes almost entirely from sewage and agricultural waste.

China is very short of arable land, so land anywhere near a watercourse is likely to have been claimed for agriculture. Part of the tillage process involves maintaining its fertility, which in other countries might involve fallow-cropping, silage, compost and various other natural techniques along with chemical fertilisers. China is much too close to subsistence. Every field must be kept in production year after year and throughout the year. Every corn stalk or rice straw must be fed to animals or used as cooking fuel. So the fields are fertilised with chemicals and with human and animal manure, and these are the substances that pollute the natural waterways and irrigation canals.

One might argue that most of this is not pollution at all, but merely the normal ecological cycle in a heavily populated land. Be that as it may, the landscape flows with dilute sewage. Chinese society knows no other order of things, and life has adapted to the situation.

The minority who live in the cities benefit from the second type of water supply: piped city water. This is certainly a great convenience, and in Gaozhou it's also clean enough to brush your teeth with. The city water in Gaozhou is piped from a large reservoir in the hills about 30 km north of the town. There are only a few rubber plantations around the reservoir and very little habitation, so the water in the reservoir is more or less pure rainwater runoff. The reservoir is a favourite swimming spot for Gold Land personnel and visitors during the summer, but we can get there only because we have access to a company truck. That means we are about the only people who visit the reservoir in this way. Although I have no test results, the water is probably as pure as in most reservoirs anywhere in the world. After the reservoir, however, there is no further purification process, so there's a continuous risk of contamination. Many Chinese think that I'm foolish even to brush my teeth with the stuff.

When a group of our managers succeeded in getting visas for a visit to Hong Kong I invited them to my house for a barbecue. I fired up my wok and popped some popcorn. That was a big hit. Then we grilled up some meat and sausages on one of our Gold

Land barbecues. They enjoyed that as well. They drank some Hong Kong beer, they tried the potato salad, but at the end of the evening the green salad was untouched. Chinese cuisine doesn't feature green salads, and when you think about their water situation it's easy to see why. Water from the city tap or the village well is quite suitable for boiling rice. And it's quite suitable for washing vegetables if those vegetables are then to be thoroughly boiled, stewed or fried. But if you crave a glass of water to drink you should be prepared to drink it hot.

As in most parts of the world, the Chinese must boil all of their water before drinking, so boiled water is the third and most tenuous of the three water supplies. In a fancy tourist hotel the water is boiled in an electric water heater. It doesn't really boil the water; it holds it just below the boiling point. But since there is a heater on every floor, the water stands in the heater for hours or even days before use. Although this wastes a bit of electricity, the long cooking leaves the water safe to drink. Restaurants run their stoves continuously and waste enough heat to boil water for an army. Sick patrons are bad for business, so they have no trouble keeping large quantities of water on the boil for long periods of time. You can certainly get sick in a Chinese restaurant, but it probably won't be from the tea. Water problems are much more likely to arise wherever water is boiled by the kettleful.

This is sometimes the case on boats and trains, and usually in offices and private homes. In private homes it's a fuel problem. Most Chinese have enough food to eat, but those in the countryside have to struggle to find fuel with which to cook it. Fossil fuels are not available, electricity is too expensive and dung is too valuable in agriculture. So in the countryside most cooking is done over what could loosely be described as wood fires. In fact, China is extremely short of wood, and harvesting actual trees is very strictly controlled. So most cooking fuel is actually leaves, twigs, dried ferns or pine needles. Old women and school-age children invest a discouraging amount of time and effort in collecting these fuels, and Chinese forests and roadsides look as if they've been swept with a broom—as indeed they often have. You can ride a bicycle through a Chinese wood. There is no underbrush, and the only cover on the bare ground might be a bit of moss. This laboriously collected fuel must be used wisely, so the different materials are sorted for fuelling slow cooking and heating fires or quick blazes of intense heat. Unfortunately, boiling drinking water sometimes falls into the quick blaze category. If you visit a Chinese home or a three-table roadside foodstall outside the normal meal hours there is a danger that they'll stoke up the fire with a bundle of dried ferns to boil up some water for your tea. This may bring the water to a passable boil, but it won't hold it there for the 15 minutes or so necessary to sterilise it. In any case, they can't keep you waiting so long for your tea. So the quality of your water falls back on the quality of their well. Good luck.

Boats and trains are not short of fuel. In fact, they often use electric water heaters like a hotel. But if they are relying on an electric kettle, you would be better advised to buy a bottle of beer. The attendant may boil the first kettle correctly, then carry it around refilling the cups and vacuum flasks of the passengers. But when the first kettle runs out, the attendant must refill it and reboil it before continuing. She may do a proper job, but don't bet your health on it.

Since most residents of Gold Land Town have no cooking facilities of their own, the factory must supply their boiled water both for home use and on the job. We have a special crew of five who start this work at 4.30 every morning. They operate a boiler fired by the same coke we use for casting. At most times of day the pressure in the city water mains is unpredictable (especially as we're at the end of the system, about 4 km outside the town), but at 4.30 a.m. it's usually good enough for them to be able to fill the boiler, boil it up and then begin distributing the water by 6.30. Distribution is by means of little water tanks mounted on wheels in the form of wheelbarrows. These tanks are filled from the boiler and then pushed by hand around to the various workshops and offices to fill vacuum flasks and jugs. The crew make regular rounds throughout the day, so households and workshops in each part of the factory know at what time to bring their containers for refilling. Homes and offices use vacuum flasks to keep the water hot for tea. But casting is hard work, and in hot weather the employees in the workshops need more liquid more quickly than they can drink in the form of hot tea. So the workshops have both an insulated urn for hot water and another pottery urn which cools its contents for quick and voluminous drinking.

This boiled water crew is a relatively efficient way to ensure the health of our employees and their dependants. But it's only one-third of Gold Land's three-part water system. Like many factories in other parts of the world we also have two piped water systems: city water and process water. City water in Gaozhou costs about 25 Chinese cents per cubic metre. That's about US$66.50 per thousand gallons, so at those prices we conserve it pretty carefully. Apart from the canteen and the water-boiling department, there are only about ten city water taps scattered around Gold Land Town. They're out in the open where everyone can keep an eye on them, and the maintenance department checks them regularly to ensure that they don't drip. Anyone is free to draw from these public taps as they see fit, and Gold Land picks up the tab. But they must bring their own pail and draw the water in view of their neighbours. In fact, the system works pretty well.

In addition to city water for drinking, a factory needs lots of other water for casting work, for tending gardens, washing trucks and so on. I learned about Gold Land's process water system one evening when I was out for a jog. The dirt tracks through the surrounding paddies provide lovely, quiet running, and in the evening there's rarely anyone out in the fields. I was surprised, therefore, to hear the familiar cry of 'General Manager!' It was Uncle Chan, a man I had always known as one of the retired workers. 'Uncle Chan, what are you doing out here?' 'I'm almost done, but the water is low at this time of year, so the weir needs constant attention.' Weir? Sure enough, not far away was a pump house beside a small stream. Uncle Chan had been literally put out to pasture tending the pump which supplies our process water from this remote stream.

Uncle Chan spends his days at the pump house about a kilometre from the factory. A power line runs from the factory to the pump house, and a pipeline runs back. The pump is not large enough to keep up with peak demands for water, so he pumps all day to fill a large open reservoir within the factory.

Some of the silt settles out here before another larger pump transfers the water up into a water tower standing above the other factory buildings.

The water tower is necessary, of course, to maintain a constant water pressure in the system. It's actually a two-part structure: the upper tank holds city water and the lower tank process water. There are two advantages to pumping city water up into our tower. In the first place, the tower ensures that residents of the factory don't experience the variations in water pressure which residents of the rest of Gaozhou take for granted. But at the same time, in our location on the outskirts of town, we can't rely on the pressure in the mains to supply enough water for our needs. The pump that fills the tower actually sucks water out of the city mains and into our factory. Even then, we have to run it all night to keep the tank full.

Modern readers of the bible may wonder at all the washing of feet that goes on. In China this preoccupation with feet washing survives today, and the reasons are the same as in biblical times: the environment is dirty, and shoes are rudimentary. Most Chinese citizens rarely set foot on an artificial surface. Even the floors of their homes are of packed clay. In the centre of most villages is a cement platform about the size of a tennis court which is used for threshing grain; in other villages this work is done on the public highways. Elsewhere, all is dirt. And, of course, most Chinese citizens work in agriculture, and the dirt in the fields is dirt of the dirtiest kind. Traditionally, the Chinese bathe each night before retiring. If they don't bathe, they must at least be sure to wash their feet.

The roads within the factory are mostly paved, and the offices have cement floors. But work in a cast iron foundry still leaves everyone ready for a shower at the end of the day. Unfortunately, the facilities at Gold Land are not really adequate. Tucked away behind a warehouse, near the water boiler, is one communal shower room with eight cubicles for the women and twelve for the men. It's made of brick with a tile roof, but there's a gap of about a metre between the roof and the top of the walls, so it's similar to the outdoor showers in a Western campground. The floors are bare cement, and the water runs out through a hole in the base of the wall, down a trough and through the factory wall to end up in a little stream in an adjoining field. The whole structure is unpainted, and each half is lit with four small light bulbs; so it's a gloomy and unappealing sort of place. Except to the mosquitoes.

In the winter, nevertheless, there's a nightly lineup outside the men's and women's doors, because the showers offer hot water. It's unusual to find hot running water in China. The villages have no plumbing of any kind, and fuel is too precious to be used to heat water for showers. Most people bathe in the irrigation canals—little boys fully nude, little girls fully clothed—or with a bucket and ladle system at home. Gold Land is able to provide hot water because we have access to large quantities of coke. The same coke-burning furnace which boils the drinking water is used to bubble steam into a large, elevated water tank. The steam heats the water, which is then piped to the shower room next door. Local basketball teams love to play at Gold Land, because after the game they get to enjoy the fruits of our coke supply.

In summer the queues for the shower room are shorter. The weather is hot, water from the tap is already almost at body temperature, and the shower room is plagued with mosquitoes. So most people send their children to bathe under the public taps, and the adults use a bucket and ladle.

Like the bathing facilities, sewage facilities are also communal. This is the normal practice in China, as most Chinese villages don't have the piped water necessary to operate individual toilet fixtures and to flush away the waste. But another reason is that in China the waste is valuable as fertiliser. The system works much like the rubbish recycling practised in some Western societies. The waste is only valuable in large quantities, so individuals are encouraged to use central common latrines to add their contributions to those of their neighbours. All over China the roadsides are dotted with brick latrines boldly labelled in giant characters to attract passersby to leave their donations to the local economy.

As with garbage recycling, it's important to segregate the different components as early as possible. Each latrine has a separate urinal. In the towns, public latrines are a nuisance and a health hazard, so the few that exist have running water and are operated by the municipality much as in other countries. But urine collection goes on in the usual way. There are privately operated public urinals along the roadsides, even in the middle of towns. These consist of a few bamboo stakes driven into the ground and hung with old jute bags, banana leaves or other material to form a small enclosure. The enclosure is just large enough to hold a large pottery urn set in the ground. The owner has only to maintain the screening, and in exchange collects a supply of high-nitrogen fertiliser.

With 800 full-time residents plus additional employees in the daytime, Gold Land is a valuable fertiliser resource for the surrounding farmland. Our showers simply drain through a hole in the factory wall and pollute the surface water with soap. But our sanitary wastes are treated much more carefully. The office area and each workshop has its own latrine. Because it's set among accommodation units, the office facility is only a urinal with a water flush. The flush is piped out through the factory wall and wasted. But each of the other workshops carefully segregates its liquid and solid waste in the usual way. In the accommodation area there's a series of urinals of the urn-and-screen kind, not so much for the value of the urine, but just to keep things orderly. In addition, there are two proper latrine blocks. Like the shower rooms, these are constructed in holiday campsite style with a gap between the brick walls and the tile roof, and inside are rows of private cubicles. Each side has water for washing the hands, but there's no flush. The latrines empty into a large pit which has an opening outside the factory wall, and every morning and evening the local farmers come and empty the pit.

This is not as nasty as it sounds, and in any case it's a normal part of every Chinese farmer's daily round. He has a special set of two black rubber pails carried on the ends of a special shoulder-carrying pole. He also has a black rubber ladle of about a litre capacity on the end of a long wooden handle. He keeps these items by his cesspit, apart from his other equipment. To fill the buckets, he needs to touch only the handle of the ladle, which is about 2 metres long, so when emptying it into the buckets he can stand well back. In picking up and carrying the two buckets, he normally needs to touch only the shoulder pole, and he tips the buckets into his cesspit with the ladle and his feet. The odour is unpleasant, but he shares this discomfort with the original user of the latrine. Which is everyone. So, unsatisfactory as other nations might find it, the system works pretty well in China. The long walk to the latrine is the worst part.

The six foundry workshops constitute the heart of Gold Land. Each foundry is arranged around a furnace used for preparing the molten iron. The furnace is a metal cylinder about 2 metres in diameter and 6 metres high and lined on the inside with refractory brick. Near the bottom an array of holes admits air supplied by a large blower to raise the temperature of the fire. It's a primitive device, with essentially no moving parts. The moulding employees start work at about 7 o'clock, but the furnace employees don't light the furnace until about lunchtime. Rice straw and firewood are used to get it going, then they begin adding coke and opening up the air supply until the furnace holds a roaring hot coke fire. After that, iron, more coke and a few minor ingredients are dumped into the open top of the furnace. The iron melts and gradually trickles down through the burning coke, undergoing some chemical changes, until it collects as a pool of molten iron in the bottom of the furnace. The furnace takes about four hours to heat up, but then more coke and iron can be added as coke is consumed and molten iron is drawn off from the bottom. An average-sized furnace makes about a tonne of molten iron per hour.

The iron is drawn off from the bottom of the furnace into a giant crucible. The gate is opened, and a stream of white-hot molten iron pours down a spillway into the crucible in a shower of sparks. The crane then transports the heavy crucible out onto the casting floor where the molten iron is decanted off a little at a time into ladles small enough for one man to carry. Working quickly, the men pour the glowing liquid from the ladles into moulds formed in the sand. Unlike the barefoot moulding employees in their ragged shorts, these employees must wear hats, gloves, goggles, heavy clothing and shoes. It's hot and heavy work in the sticky heat of south China.

We make our cast iron products by a simple and old-fashioned technique known as sand casting. We first mould a hole in the ground in the shape of the finished piece, then pour the molten iron into the hole. When the iron has cooled we dig it up.

In order to mould the cavity in the correct shape, the dirt must have just the right consistency. The composition is based primarily on sand mixed with a bit of clay, coal powder and just the right amount of moisture. Each sand mould can make only one piece, and it's destroyed when the piece is dug up. So to maintain a high output, we need to make many identical sand moulds, each of which takes up a little square of floor space. On entering one of the foundries the first impression is of a vast, empty room. The floor is entirely covered with sand, and because the sand contains coal powder the floor is black. This gives the entire vast space a grim, dark air. Overhead, a crane rumbles back and forth transporting hoppers of sand or ladles of glowing molten iron.

During most of the day, dozens of men and women work singly or in pairs scattered over the casting floor. These are the moulding employees. Each team or individual has a pile of sand, a shovel and a plastic pattern of the product he is making mounted in a moulding box. His job is conceptually quite simple. He rams sand into the moulding box, then places the assembly on the floor. The box is constructed in such a way that both it and the plastic pattern can be removed, leaving a block of sand with a cavity inside in the shape of the product. Holes in the assembly allow molten iron to be poured into the cavity and air to escape. Each team is assigned an area of floor space and asked to cover it with moulds before going home.

Although our products are sold in Western markets this is definitely not a Western foundry. There are no lift trucks, for example. Everything at Gold Land is transported in carts a bit like wheelbarrows. There are no hard hats, and little other safety equipment. But for a Western visitor the most striking feature of this sizeable factory is that there is no parking lot. China is modernising, but there is still a long way to go.

3

Filling the iron rice bowl

IN a Chinese enterprise, the Personnel Manager has a complex job. The People's Republic has tried to create an 'iron rice bowl' for its workers, using each according to his abilities and providing for each according to his needs. The result, as in every communist state, has been a vast and ineffective state planning apparatus and a tangle of social welfare policies and regulations. Unfortunately, conventional dogma calls for all of this to be distributed, applied and followed up through the work unit. So down at the sharp end, someone in the factory must try to interpret the policies of the welfare state and apply them to the inconvenient realities of the lives of human beings; all the while trying to maintain peace and harmony in the workplace. It's not surprising that in most factories the General Manager spends a lot of his time on personnel matters. At Gold Land, however, I'm quite incompetent even to appreciate the full ramifications of the iron rice bowl, much less to administer its complex political component. So most of this work falls to the unlucky Personnel and Administration Manager.

Mr So Lui Mo is a quiet, easy-going sort. The new joint venture has brought a lot of change and uncertainty to his job, but he always has a cheery greeting and a smile. His wife works on the casting floor, and they live in a modest factory housing unit with their single young son. Nice people.

Too nice, in fact. Mr So is the kind of manager who is so

35

anxious to be helpful that he'll make every effort to avoid ever actually saying no. It's easy to imagine how he developed this flexibility of character. The many political campaigns that have swept through Chinese society in recent decades have required loyal party members to support first this faction and then another at the behest of the central authorities. Mr So is certainly a loyal party member. His job demands it, for the Personnel and Administration Manager is the main administrative point of contact between government policies and the lives of those assigned to the work unit. If there is to be a crackdown on birth-control violators, a purge of unauthorised peasants in industry or just another consciousness-raising campaign, Mr So is the man who must make it happen in the foundry. He's been doing it effectively for years, and yet has remained well liked within the work unit.

Mr Chow is the Chairman of our Board of Directors, and he is supported by Mr Chin. Both are paid by Gold Land, but Mr Chin's particular responsibility is to represent the Communist Party in the board's deliberations. Among the operating managers, Mr So is in charge of personnel matters, but his work too is watched over by a counterpart: our union leader, Mr Ho Wing Nam. All four of these men are trusted senior party members. At the same time, all four work loyally in the interests of Gold Land. This doubling-up is standard operating procedure in any Leninist society, and it's a clear reminder that despite his emollient personality, Mr So is a powerful man.

To understand Mr So's job, it's first necessary to understand China's remarkable class system. The central planners have at their disposal a 700 million-strong labour force. The planners must come to grips with channelling and applying this force in a way that will generate the greatest output from the economy. It's a daunting task. As a first step, they invoke assistance from Marxist fundamentals and divide the labour force into two broad classes: workers and peasants.

Chinese society has in fact five classes, but the 'peasants' and the 'workers' account for 99 per cent of the population. About 85 per cent of Chinese citizens are officially classed as peasants; almost everyone else is a worker. Peasants live in the country, workers live in towns; most peasants work in some capacity related to agriculture, workers normally do not.

These two classes are exclusive (you can't be both a peasant and a worker) and there is little inter-class mobility. Class status is not officially supposed to be hereditary, and in fact it's one of the pillars of Chinese social justice that each child should be guided into an adult role suited to his abilities. But in reality most Chinese belong to the same class as their parents, though there is a gradual one-way flow. Workers are generally considered to have higher status than peasants. Particularly able peasant children can grow up to be workers, while adults with worker status make certain by whatever means that their children will never be classified as peasants.

Co-existing with these two major classes are three much smaller ones, and this is where the complications begin. The easiest of these three to understand is the 'soldier' class. The title includes officers as well as enlisted men, and sailors and airmen as well as soldiers. This is a class you can join and leave, but again it's exclusive. While you're a soldier, you lose your previous class designation. Many places and institutions in China are named the 'Workers, Peasants and Soldiers ... ' park, auditorium or whatever. The army class serves as an important route for peasant boys who aspire to become workers. If they can learn a valuable industrial skill during their army service they can become eligible for jobs in industry with worker status. (In practice, this is a rare accomplishment, but truck driving is one example. Until recently, most truck drivers were army-trained.)

The 'leader' class is the nobility of the Chinese class system. Every institution has its quota of leader positions—at Gold Land we have four for a workforce of 1000. It's an *ex-officio* membership: whoever is appointed to be Gold Land's Assistant General Manager can call himself a leader. His work record will acknowledge this status, and he'll receive various improvements in his state-supplied benefits. Since every sort of work unit has leaders, there are peasant leaders as well as worker leaders. The Communist Party also appoints leaders, although they normally work full time for the party, so the party is their work unit. A company like Gold Land is not likely to find itself suddenly with a fifth leader who is important in the party but works for us as a truck driver. In government work units, however, this can sometimes occur.

The final class designation is the thorny 'cadre'. This class has no obvious parallel in the West, and after a couple of years of poking at it I'm still not sure that I understand all its ramifications. I usually think of a cadre as the Chinese version of the British MBE: he bears an honour bestowed by the government in recognition of merit, but his accomplishments may have been in almost any sphere of Chinese life. The difference is that China bestows many more of these honours than does Queen Elizabeth, distributes them much more extensively through society and attaches greater practical benefits. Leaders are always appointed from the ranks of the cadres, so all leaders are also cadres in the sense that all billionaires are also millionaires. (Though a Chinese would immediately point me out as a leader who is not a cadre.)

The most straightforward way to become a cadre is to graduate from a university. Graduates are automatically appointed cadres. In early 1990 rumours circulated that there would be a weeding out of unqualified cadres. If this happens, it will probably be aimed at blocking 1989's student protestors from enjoying cadre status. People can also qualify for cadre status through distinguished army service or outstanding service in the Communist Party. The cadre designation overlaps all the other groups, so a cadre's identity papers will mention that he's a cadre, but also state that he belongs to one of the other four classes.

Gold Land's workforce contains more than 100 cadres. In addition to the leaders all the managers are cadres, and we have a few young university graduates. We support some retired cadres, as well as some people who used to be managers who have now been demoted to lesser jobs but who remain cadres. And the rest are people who earned their cadre status outside the foundry, in either the party or the army. We have lots of truck-driving, sand-shovelling and vegetable-washing cadres of whom I'm not even aware. Schoolteacher cadres often haven't enough cash for their next pair of shoes. Many a peasant cadre can't speak the national language or sign his name.

The cadre title is most often used by retirees who no longer have a work assignment and fall back on their cadre status as the most favourable description of their place in society. It's such a catch-all class that I find it hard to understand why it exists. But cadres do get various special privileges. The most visible is their right to ride in the soft carriages of trains. Anyone who is not a cadre can do so only by paying for the ticket with Foreign Exchange Certificates. Many Westerners assume from the original French meaning of the word that all cadres must be Communist Party members. It's not so.

If you want to visualise the Chinese social hierarchy, begin by imagining a pie. Cut it in three slices: 85 per cent peasants, 14.5 per cent workers and a sliver for the army. Now draw a smaller pie in the centre (say 15 per cent of the whole) to show the cadres overlapping all three other groups. Finally, in the centre of that draw the tiniest circle you can manage to show the leaders.

In principle, central planning should try to organise the activities of both the peasants and the workers, but in practice most of the effort is focused on the couple of hundred million workers. The hundreds of millions of peasants are just too numerous, too scattered, too illiterate and too conservative to be amenable to much control. They are also too vital. Various collectivisations and other reforms of agriculture have been tried in the past, and the result was decreased output. So as a rule the peasants are simply registered as a member of a particular village, given an output quota and left to get on with it.

The planner is now free to manage his 'worker' resources much more intensively. Ideally, I suppose, they should be managed individually, with each worker tested, trained and fitted to his ideal employment. But anyone who has seen the armed forces' attempts at this kind of manpower management knows that the working alternative to a free-choice job market has not yet been invented. So the central planner makes another gross simplification and groups the workers by geographical area. Each worker is normally born, raised, educated and employed within a particular county. Each county has its birth-control bureaucracy, residence registration roll and educational system. And at the conclusion of middle school each worker becomes the responsibility of the county Labour Bureau or, if he has some specialised training, of its counterpart, the Employment Bureau.

At this level the numbers are small enough that each worker can be treated, at least for some purposes, as an individual. The Labour Bureau consults with the local industries to find jobs for new graduates. In some cases this amounts to a real placement exercise, but the default option is that new workers who remain unplaced are directed to the work units of their parents. Eventually, when the workers are given their first assignment, the bureau turns them over to the Personnel Manager of the work unit. Mr So then takes control of many aspects of a Gold Land worker's life.

A couple of other systems have been designed to work in parallel with central labour planning, but they fail to take into account the real-life complications. In a communist society, the party has a parallel structure which mirrors all the other institutions of society. So each work unit (factory, restaurant, monastic order) should have a small proportion of party members in its ranks who function rather like school prefects. Not all party members hold senior jobs, and not all cadres and leaders are party members. But the party members spend extra time studying the latest nuances of party policy and ensure that their party superiors are aware of any non-conformist behaviour within their work unit. Membership and advancement in the party are outside the scope of work unit management. If party members within the factory object to something they would normally apply pressure only upward through party channels (Mr Ho and Mr Chin) to the government and then back down from the government to Mr Chow and to me. In fact, I can't say much more about the party, because within Gold Land its activities have been rather inconspicuous and I prefer to let this particular sleeping dog lie.

Apart from the party, the other big influence on Mr So's work could potentially be Mr Ho Wing Nam and the union. Mr So and Mr Ho have always succeeded in maintaining harmonious relations between the company and the union, so I have never had occasion to probe too deeply into what's going on. It certainly helps, however, that both Mr Ho and Mr Chin describe the union's function as 'helping management in promoting production'. There is also a clear policy of 'no strikes' which is said to have originated in Beijing with the Central Committee of the Communist Party.

Both Mr Ho and his assistant, Mrs Tong Mun Yue, are paid, housed and otherwise supported by Gold Land, but they are actually employees of the provincial union organisation, not employees of our company. Mrs Tong was promoted to her post from among our workforce, but Mr Ho came to the foundry about three years ago from another factory in Gaozhou. Both of them are party members, which I assume must be a prerequisite for this type of work. The union leaders receive separate training and non-monetary rewards through their union connections. They go on union-organised training courses and receive their own versions of government policy documents on labour regulations and related matters.

At Gold Land we have been able to turn over to Mr Ho and Mrs Tong all the headaches of housing assignments, the library, the canteen and all sorts of benefit programmes. In addition, they organise various annual gifts to the workforce, medical checkups, and Mrs Tong is in charge of the birth-control programme.

After the joint venture's first year, our union was named a Model Union, a rating granted to only 3 per cent of all work units. The only obvious perquisites of this honour were a banner to hang in our union office, a flood of inquiring visitors who came to 'study our situation' (and to stay for lunch) and a one-month training course in Beijing for Mrs Tong (at Gold Land's expense).

As each new recruit is assigned to the work unit Mr So creates that person's work record file. Superficially, it's much like a personnel file anywhere. It's confidential, and it contains the person's entire work history, salary record and disciplinary record. An employee is careful to keep his work file unblemished, as he is not supposed to have any means of shaking off his past. He is not supposed to have the possibility of resigning his post and starting over with a clean slate in a new work unit. And the file

41

is not just a work file. It is society's record of that person's life. It records, for example, any problems with the police, domestic difficulties and compliance with the birth-control policies. Should an employee ever apply for privileges such as a passport, party membership or better housing, this is the file that will be consulted and this is where the results will be recorded. So the personnel files are the Personnel Manager's most talked-about responsibility.

In recent years it has become more and more difficult for personnel managers to implement the schemes of the central planners, as the whole labour-planning edifice has been progressively falling apart. It worked well enough as long as a worker assigned to our work unit had almost no possibility of ever leaving it. In those days, the state provided the worker's food, clothing and housing through the work unit. His residence registration was through the work unit. Anyone leaving his work unit would have become a homeless beggar until he was picked up by the Public Security Bureau (call it the police) and brought back to his original work unit for re-education. Any gentle soul who found himself assigned for life to a cast iron foundry when he was hoping for a career singing Chinese opera would have had only one means of escape short of suicide (itself a crime, incidentally)—he might somehow have convinced the Labour Bureau that a mistake had been made which must be rectified for the good of society and the nation. How he might have convinced them is not spelled out in the realm of principle; in the realm of practice it came down to friends, influence and payoffs.

If the system still worked this way Mr So's life would indeed be much easier than it is in these progressive times. For in recent years the 'open policies', in an effort to accelerate modernisation of the economy, have created some new categories of employment which effectively scrap most of the old labour-planning mechanisms.

In order to attract foreign technology and management knowhow China now allows foreign firms to set up joint ventures, or even wholly owned subsidiaries. Gold Land is a particular type of joint venture, a relatively unpopular type, based on an existing government-owned work unit. The term of our initial joint-venture contract is ten years. The Chinese partner (the Gaozhou government) contributes the foundry site, buildings, equipment, goodwill and its captive workforce as its part of the venture. The Hong Kong partner agrees to invest at least a certain amount of hard currency in improving the factory, and to provide foreign management expertise: me. During the ten years they share the risks and profits, and the foreign partner gets firm control of a cheap Chinese source of supply for its worldwide distribution business. At the end of the term the improved factory and retrained workforce revert to government control.

This by itself is pretty straightforward and need not upset the central planning apple-cart. China is lending partial control of Mr So and his 1000 employees to the joint venture for ten years, and after that they will all revert to the ambit of the central planners; the joint venture is just an interlude. But China wants to move into avionics and computer peripherals, where they have no established factories to contribute. These industries call for joint ventures of another type which must be set up from scratch. Everyone intends that these newly created ventures will be permanent additions to the economy, but officially they too are set up under five-, ten- or fifteen-year contracts. If the venture should then be abandoned the employees have no predecessor work unit to return to. In addition, the foreign investors in these new work units have insisted that since new staff are to be recruited they should have the power to select, discipline and, if necessary, dismiss them.

These newly created enterprises are clearly a much riskier proposition from the employees' point of view. They want to be compensated for the lack of a guaranteed future with better pay, at rates beyond the national scale. And these mobile employees blow a hole in the central assignment of labour. In fact, they really can't be staffed by central planning at all. They are staffed by standard Hong Kong techniques: posters in the street.

With this going on, it's clear that our frustrated opera singer need no longer tax his valued larynx with the dusty air of a cast iron foundry. For the price of a bus ticket he can pack his meagre possessions off to the greener pastures of one of the new electronics companies, a bank or even the hotel trade. He can leave his personnel file and all the blind injustices of central planning behind him. It's a risky and exciting step, but he can slip the net and swim free in the fast-flowing waters of the market economy.

Gold Land's permanent workers will have a state unit to return to at the end of the joint venture's term, so we could, if we so desired, continue to call on central planning to staff our foundry. We decline to do so, because we would lose the power to select and dismiss the people they send us. Unfortunately, it must be admitted that in China, as anywhere else, a cast iron foundry is one of the less desirable working environments. The new opportunities for social mobility have drained off our workforce, and Mr So is forced to devote a lot of effort to replenishing it, including taking in more and more underemployed peasant farmers from the surrounding villages. These unofficial 'workers' now make up more than half of our labour force.

Meanwhile, other developments have been undermining the labour-allocation system from another angle. In the mid-1980s, as an experiment, certain state enterprises (including the Gaozhou Foundry) were given authority to implement performance-related pay. Normally, pay is based almost entirely on educational level and seniority. Inserting a performance element complicated life for Mr So and for the Payroll Department, but it also opened up the question of pay levels among the employees.

Previously, there had been little to discuss. Pay levels were derisory, but the necessities were supplied. Everyone was perpetually skint, but there was nothing much to buy. Once the economy began to open up, goods worth buying began appearing in the shops. All at once the workforce became much more interested in cash compensation. Lifetime employment and the iron rice bowl became benefits to be evaluated rather than simply a system to be accepted. But performance-related pay was only the first step.

Certain work units, including Gaozhou Foundry, were put on a 'contract responsibility system'. This system had only just been introduced when the joint venture took over the foundry. The concept was to introduce a note of enterprise into state-owned enterprises by placing full control in the hands of the Factory

Director, with an attractive profit-sharing bonus as his incentive. In theory, one of his prerogatives was to reduce the workforce, though in practice he was rarely allowed to exercise it. Faced with the possibility that the iron rice bowl could be broken, and being underemployed anyway, many people took a flyer at that sinful mystery called private enterprise. During the lunch break and after hours, people began cutting hair, washing trucks and selling things on the street. Once the private economy was in operation and shown to be working, the barriers were down. Lifetime employment became optional, and labour allocation became labour forecasting.

Gold Land has seven personnel and administration staff, including the two union representatives. As in any firm any-where, one of their major preoccupations is pay. Our pay scheme is a rather unusual one devised by the foundry when it was originally authorised to experiment with performance-related pay. The majority of the employees are paid pure piecework and, with the co-operation of the union, this works rather well.

Each piece we manufacture is cast, machined, painted and packed in a series of specialised workshops. On the basis of experience and educated guesswork each workshop is offered a certain fee for completing its part of the process on each piece. Mr Go must assure that each workshop is scheduled a mix of pieces each month that will earn a total sum adequate for the size of the shop's staff. Within the workshop the foreman then divides the work to be done on a particular item into its com-ponent operations and divides up the piecerate in proportion to the difficulty of each task. If he does this well he knows that he can then assign employees to tasks freely, because an individual can earn approximately the same total pay cheque whether the task is easy or difficult.

For most employees this is the entire pay system. There is no guaranteed minimum, no overtime and no ceiling. So, to a cer-tain extent, employees can set their own hours. Some co-ordination is required, of course. But if a woman needs to take a longer lunch to visit her child's teacher it's normally not a prob-lem; her absence affects only her own earnings. An employee in particular need of money can earn as much as he's willing to work for. The highest monthly pay cheques in the company go not to the managers, but to the most diligent of the production employees. But the most striking feature of this system in the Chinese context is that all employees are treated alike. Peasants and workers are paid on the same piecerates, and the man or woman who produces the most takes home the most money regardless of his or her social class. An employee who produces nothing gets nothing, whatever class he may be.

This radically simple system drastically reduces the tea drinking, water-pipe smoking and newspaper reading that are the curse of most Chinese factories. And at the same time it reduces the need for supervisory staff to keep people moving.

However, to obtain these benefits, we pay a price in discipline. Each employee is his own boss, and in certain situations—when the power is off, for example—he may decide that it's not worth his while to report for work. Everyone works part time, and as the work is hot and heavy most people set themselves a target of making a certain number of pieces and then reward themselves by stopping for a smoke or knocking off for the day. We operate an attendance bonus to make sure that it's always worthwhile to turn up for work. Everyone gets a small fixed sum for each day they report to work. Again, this applies equally to all classes.

This whole concept is a mockery of socialism; a mockery amplified by the undeniable fact that it works so well. It raises the productivity of our labour (in fact, the state's labour) and it puts money in the pockets of the employees. Joint ventures are obliged by law to ensure that their workers earn 20 per cent more than workers in state enterprises, and this system does that easily. But it has led us into trouble with another state policy. In an effort to reduce disparities and restrain inflation, firms participating in the performance-related pay experiment were asked to hold back 20 per cent of their wage bill and put it in a salary reserve fund instead of paying it out to the employees. With pure piecework this kind of manipulation is impossible, as every employee has calculated for himself how much he has coming at the end of the month. Mr So could only ignore that directive, and so far we seem to have got away with it.

About 15 per cent of the workforce doesn't earn piecework.

These are the cooks, the engineers, the truck drivers, the book-keepers and so on. These people are paid in two parts: a small basic salary and a much larger bonus. The bonus is calculated as a percentage of the average piecework earnings of all the piecerate employees in the factory. Each of these non-production jobs is rated and receives 50 to 150 per cent of the factory's overall average piecework payment. Mr So himself, for example, is on 120 per cent. This means that his monthly pay cheque rises and falls with the factory's output.

An employee's basic salary is small compared to his bonus, and much simpler to determine, as this portion is calculated on the standard central planning system for rewarding workers (official worker-class workers) all over the country. This standard system is predictably egalitarian. A new worker begins his career at the bottom of a ladder which has only three or four steps between his own starting position and the Factory Director's job. Within each step there are between three and five salary grades. So a new worker can look forward to up to fifteen promotions and raises in his career if he goes all the way to Factory Director. The salary at the top is a bit more than double that at the bottom, but position on the ladder also determines other non-salary benefits such as quality of housing and retirement benefits.

Chinese factory directors, especially those who have signed a responsibility contract, like to keep personal control over all aspects of the company's operations. But promotions are an exception. Promotions (including the Factory Director's own) are handled by the union.

Each year Mr So must negotiate with the local Economic Committee, a government organ which supervises the local factories, for a quota of promotions. In recent years the Gaozhou Foundry has been getting 3 per cent. This means that 3 per cent of the official workers can be promoted one salary grade. At that rate the average worker would get a raise once every 33 years, or perhaps once in his career. With that kind of progression the whole system becomes meaningless, so the practice has developed of offering half-grade increases. This creates twice as many promotions to distribute, but each promotion is worth only half the normal salary increase. This expedient isn't officially authorised, but it seems to be widely practised around Gaozhou.

Once the number of promotions has been negotiated the union has an elaborate 'three poster' system for deciding who receives them. Our 450 official workers entitle us to about 14 promotions, or 28 half-promotions. That works out to about two for each workshop and department, so each is given a quota roughly proportional to the number of its employees. The members of the workshop (again, this should be only the official workers, not the peasants) then get together and, under the guidance of the foreman and the party secretary, put forward a list of candidates with about twice as many names as the number of available promotions. The lists are vetted by a committee composed of Mr So, the union leaders, some party types and a few managers. They select a first list of 28 names which is posted up for all to see. There is a consultation period during which anyone (including, in principle, a peasant) who has any opinion about the selections can bring it up publicly or to the ear of Mr So, a union leader or his party secretary. There are never any such comments, but in theory these comments are used to modify the list and the committee then posts it again. This list is then submitted to the county Economic Committee for ratification, after which the names of the lucky winners are finally posted for everyone's information. Mr So notes the glad event in each one's file, and if we were not operating the piecework pay system he would then receive an absolutely derisory increment to his monthly salary. A half-grade increase would be worth about 5 yuan per month in a pay packet that fluctuates between 150 and 250 yuan for most employees.

Gold Land continues to go through this annual ritual for its 450 official workers just because no one can be sure what the future will bring. For the present, the increase is just a note in the worker's file, and his pay is calculated on his piecework as before. If strict central planning returns, the promoted workers may find a lot of social benefits tied to those meagre half-grade increases, but for the time being this is just a charade in Gold Land. Not so in a traditional state enterprise. For those employees, the iron rod of discipline is embodied in this limp noodle of a system. A lazy or undisciplined employee can't be fired or demoted. The only real sanction is to withhold his promotion when his turn comes up for inclusion in the annual 3 per cent.

It's not surprising that many Chinese workers drink a lot of tea. Gold Land's discipline problems are of a much milder sort. In theory, we are even able to dismiss redundant (permanent) workers, though we have never succeeded in actually doing so. Anyone in an office job who isn't pulling his weight can simply be transferred to a piecework position. Anyone in a piecework position must work or he gets no pay. Our biggest discipline problem, in fact, is not the conventional sleeping cadre. It's the permanent worker who operates a market stall or other private business on the side. In some cases a worker can rationally calculate that it maximises his income to work part time in the factory, enjoying our accommodation and the security and fringe benefits of a state employee, while devoting a large part of his time to a private business. From a practical point of view it's hard to fault his calculations. We would discharge a peasant for this kind of behaviour, but with a permanent worker we can only set the attendance bonus high enough to weigh heavily in his calculations. Right now, it's calculated on a daily basis, but we may have to make some provision where a certain pattern of absence forfeits the whole month.

We also have on the books a rather Draconian system of fines which can be invoked against various forms of antisocial behaviour. They are not often levied, because Chinese society very effectively censures antisocial behaviour from childhood, but these fines are one discretionary tool for enforcing discipline. Gold Land's system of fines mentions things like breaking tools through misuse, damage caused by improper care of company property and that sort of thing. The situations rarely arise. The one which is invoked most frequently is, to my mind, the least defensible. This is the Chinese tradition of fining those who are responsible for an accident. The logic behind it seems to be that workers are the state's productive resources, just like forests, factories or vehicles. So anyone injuring a state worker is damaging state property and should be fined. Carrying the logic to its conclusion, the fine applies even if the guilty party injures himself. He's fined for mangling his own hand in a machine.

At Gold Land I'm the guy who imposes these fines, and I can go along with the system in the case of safety violations. If a

49

man is pouring molten iron in his bare feet we send him home to get his shoes, and during that time he's losing money. I find that fair enough. But one day we had a mechanic repairing a machine when someone came along and turned it on. The local Safety Bureau investigated the accident and in due course fined Gold Land for poor safety practices. True enough, we hadn't provided a tag and a procedure to lock the machine 'off' while under repair. But the proposal from our Gold Land Safety Officer was that the fine should be passed on to the employee who turned on the machine, to his supervisor and to the injured mechanic. I get a proposal like this in every accident case, and once again I declined to approve it. But the staff don't understand my explanations.

Fines can be applied to enforce discipline only in these special situations. Without fines our quiver of disciplinary measures would be stocked mainly with some quaintly Maoist sanctions based on group pressure. Officially, disciplinary action against a permanent worker involves three formal steps. The first is a verbal warning. This is requested by the worker's supervisor and is administered by Mr So over a cup of tea. Most Western firms do the same before deciding to fire a difficult employee, but Mr So does it so mildly that I'm never sure if the employee understands what's going on.

The next step is a written warning. I issue these in the name of the company, society and all decent persons everywhere. A Chinese worker would normally receive very few personal letters in his entire lifetime, so this is an impressive measure. If the employee remains unimpressed, however, the final step is rather a damp squib. Mr So places an official and indelible note in the employee's file. He has officially become a defective piece in the state's vast stock of labour resources. I suppose the adverse note can later influence his child's admission to the party's junior legions or something, but it's not well designed to have immediate or practical effect on the employee's behaviour.

Less than half of our workforce are permanent workers inherited from the old foundry. If you were to draw up an honour roll of our most devoted and loyal employees, probably most of the names would be from this minority group. If you were to list the most diligent and energetic employees, the permanent workers would again be disproportionately represented—more than half the names, perhaps. But if you were to make a list of all the laziest, least productive and most troublesome employees, every one would be a permanent worker. As a joint venture we can only be thankful that we have the peasants to carry this bunch along.

In appreciation, Gold Land has gone rather out on a limb in offering to peasants benefits that are normally reserved for workers. For example, Chinese workers are not normally entitled to an annual vacation. Most factories close for a week or more at the lunar New Year, and there are three or four holidays through the year associated with patriotic themes: National Day, Army Day and a few others. On these days central planning allows for the closing of most enterprises while the various elements of the iron rice bowl, including pay, carry on. So these are genuine paid holidays. People compelled to work on these days take another day off in lieu, though there's no system of time-and-a-half that I'm aware of. When peasants illegally began to take jobs in industry they were initially hired as casual labourers and were paid by the day. On holidays they were not engaged, and so were not paid. These casual labourers gradually became valuable long-term employees and the backbone of the workforce, but the payroll calculation remained the same. So on National Day they were invited to take a rest and celebrate at their own expense. In an attempt to alleviate this discrimination we've created a fictional basic wage for our peasants equal to what would be the basic wage of a comparable official worker, and on public holidays we pay them this small sum just to put everyone on a similar footing.

Central planning empowers the Personnel Manager to grant specific amounts of personal leave to employees in certain circumstances. Deaths in the family are one example. Newlyweds get a week off, and there is carefully prescribed time off for childbirth and nursing. This birth leave is particularly tricky because it's tied in with the birth-control policy. Three months' leave is available only for the first baby in the family. For subsequent arrivals, if any, the mother gets only a few days. On the other hand, if the husband submits to sterilisation after the first birth his wife's birth leave is extended to half a year. (This isn't considered much of a bargain, and male sterilisation remains emphatically unpopular.) As the manager of the state's labour resources Mr So verifies and documents all this and justifies everything in reports to the local Labour Bureau. Again, we've extended this benefit to our peasants, but it's not often claimed. Peasants often prefer to conceal their pregnancies.

Quite a variety of situations are considered to justify a worker taking time off. Deep in the pages of small print there's even something that resembles a conventional vacation. It's called 'visiting relatives leave', and permanent employees can apply for 30 days of it once every four years. But the central planners leave nothing to the employee's absolute discretion. This one is qualified by geography and is available only to workers whose family homes are more than 50 km from their work unit. Those who live closer are presumed to be able to get in enough visiting on Sundays.

It sounds incredible that peasants should be expected to take time off without pay when they want to go to a funeral, get married or deliver a baby; especially so when the regular workers are compensated. But this injustice is more theoretical than financial since, on days off, no one earns a bonus. The only money in question is the basic wage, and basic wages are so minimal that even a Chinese employee can't take them too seriously. One day's wage for a typical factory employee is only one or two yuan, which won't even buy a packet of cigarettes. So what seems at first a glaring inequity doesn't in practice cause any obvious discontent. But by the same token, it's the pitifully low level of the basic wage which has allowed us to do something about it. We normally have to pay it only on public holidays and for special leaves, and it's so low we can afford to extend it to the peasants just to put everyone on the same basis.

Sick leave is another major problem for the Chinese Personnel Manager, just as it is for his counterpart elsewhere. State workers have the right to unlimited sick leave, so in most factories the Personnel Manager must operate an elaborate system of doctors' permission slips in order to keep absences under control. Our foundry has less of a problem, because on sick days employees receive only their basic wages. This is so far from their normal pay that it constitutes a strong deterrent. Here again, peasants should not normally be paid anything on sick days, but we extended the benefit to them in the interests of minimising class distinctions. It costs us little unless the government at some point mandates a big increase in basic wages.

Much more serious is the medicine subsidy. This is just one of the myriad little payments that, taken together, form an important part of the iron rice bowl system. In principle, work units should supply medicine to their sick (state permanent) workers. Different units discharge this responsibility in different ways. It seems that at various times in the past the Gaozhou Foundry tried them all. At one point it provided free medicine only through its own clinic, then through an approved list of dispensaries, then against a doctor's note, and at other times against official receipts. Every system was widely abused, as it is in every society. By the time we launched Gold Land, the medical subsidy had degenerated into simple but silly twice-annual flat payments. The payment was graded by age, so older and retired workers got a bit more; but it was paid out to everyone at the end of June and December and was used to buy school books and winter clothes. The medical insurance function was lost. When we extended this benefit to our peasant employees we revised it yet again and tried to restrict it to its original purpose of relieving medical expenses. This provides a good example of the practical problems of trying to operate a welfare state in a society without paper and pens.

Mr So's catalogue of benefits seems endless. In my second year on the job I was still discovering new benefits I had overlooked the first time around. In hot weather, for example, a hot soup of sugar syrup and beans is distributed in the workshops to raise the employees' spirits and to fortify their health in keeping with the Taoist theories of yin and yang. The company also gives the employees presents on various occasions. At the Mid-Autumn Festival there are special 'moon cakes', and at the lunar New Year we slaughter the pigs that dispose of our dining hall garbage and distribute the meat to the employees. At the end of the year the government asks us to name about 60 per cent of all the employees as 'Advanced Workers'. There are advanced workers, advanced party members, advanced cadres and so on. These people receive various merchandise gifts: towels, a pail, some sugar. We have an annual party for our army veterans, and on Women's Day the women get a party and some gifts. New parents get a gift of baby supplies (first child only, but an extra quantity if the father has been sterilised after the birth), and nurses give every woman a twice-annual health check. In fact, this is basically a birth-control check. When I proposed extending this benefit to the peasants Mrs Tong chuckled. 'Do you want them all to quit? This is a benefit the peasants would rather do without.'

This is the welfare state—the iron rice bowl. It would have a certain logic if only it were well administered and applied to the whole population rather than just the state's worker class. In the course of revising the benefits system I had many opportunities to discuss the inequities with Mr So, Mr Chin and Mr Ho. They had never really considered them unjust, but pointed out in mitigation that peasants have certain advantages over workers. They are more their own master, being less constrained by government policy, particularly in the matter of birth control. They live in villages of only a few extended families who can co-operate to ignore or even defy many government prescriptions. And these days peasants can even work in public or private businesses almost as if they were workers, but they can come and go as they please. At the time of the Tiananmen Square massacre in 1989, others in the factory pointed out that if turmoil returns to Chinese society the peasants can retreat to their village and carry on much as before, leaving their worker compatriots to bear the brunt of purges, crackdowns and re-education. To hear the workers tell it, peasant status has a lot to recommend it. And I'm told that most of the big earners running Guangdong's private enterprises and working in the new joint ventures are peasants who were free to take a chance, break free and seek their fortunes in the new economic environment.

I must confess that neither the workers nor the peasants were much impressed by my efforts to erase the class distinctions within Gold Land. The whole project was a big headache to Mr So, who spent hours explaining my radical schemes to the government. To his surprise, although the government couldn't understand why we would want to equalise their benefits, they allowed that if we wanted to throw away our money they had no objection. In the factory the announcement of the changes was received with only mild interest. And at the end of the year, when Mr So and Mr Chin prepared our submission to be declared an Advanced Work Unit, our new benefit regulations were not one of the arguments used to support our case.

Nevertheless, I'm convinced that the class system cannot survive for long. If the class distinctions don't destroy it, the accounting will. Because from what I've seen the Chinese welfare state seems to be erected on a crumbling foundation of unfunded liabilities.

Chinese bookkeeping is never strong on accruals or amortisations, but this is particularly evident in the case of pensions. The iron rice bowl, of course, extends from the cradle to the grave, so a state enterprise with a 30-year history like the Gaozhou Foundry has about 10 per cent retired workers on its payroll who are entitled to a reduced salary plus all the usual benefits and a few special ones besides. Mr So takes care of all the administration, but it's the General Manager who has to worry about where the money will come from. If the company is prosperous, all is well. Under the old system, if the work unit was failing the state would support it with special grants. But a joint venture doesn't have the state to fall back on. Many joint ventures are not even meeting their payrolls, much less funding medical, pension and other liabilities.

Every personnel manager's biggest unfunded liability is his obligation to pay a lot of unnecessary workers for the rest of their lives. In China as a whole, state enterprises are estimated to harbour somewhere between 15 and 20 million of them. In recent years, as some of the state enterprises have been turned into joint ventures or contracted out under the contract responsibility system, the new managements have begun looking for ways to relieve this burden.

On one occasion, one of our mechanics was hospitalised by an industrial accident. In Chinese hospitals it's traditional for a family member to stay in the hospital with the patient and to take care of the basic nursing. The mechanic's wife worked in a state-owned restaurant which had recently been contracted out under the responsibility system, so Mr So went to see the manager of the restaurant to arrange some time off for the mechanic's wife.

The restaurant was grossly overstaffed. As at Gold Land, the manager had inherited the full staff of the previous state restaurant when he signed his responsibility contract and he should have been happy to have the mechanic's wife away from work for a few weeks, especially as Gold Land offered to pay for her various benefits while she was away. The restaurant manager, however, wouldn't agree. He was playing for higher stakes. He was hoping that the mechanic's case might be serious enough that the wife would begin taking unauthorised time off. If her nursing duties kept her away long enough he might be able to delete her from his roster and send her name back to the Labour Bureau for reassignment. In fact, the Labour Bureau would be reluctant to apply the rules in such a case, but the actual outcome might well depend on certain advantages offered to officials of the Labour Bureau by one party or the other.

There was no suggestion that the mechanic's wife was a poor employee, but if she ever found her name on the waiting-for-work roll at the Labour Bureau she might be a long while restoring her reputation. With all the security and fringe benefits involved, a Chinese worker will fight hard to keep his iron rice bowl. There's a presumption that anyone who has been returned for reassignment against his will must at the very least have molested his factory director's under-age daughter. The Labour Bureau realises that its image as an employment exchange has degenerated to this extent (it knows all too well the catalogue of offences attributed to the flotsam returned to its unassigned pool), so the bureau helps to protect the innocent by refusing to take them back. Mr So explained these facts of life to the new restaurant manager, and in the end we were able to borrow the mechanic's wife in exchange for a monthly cash payment.

This same concern for preserving the status of state workers tripped us up again on another occasion. When we learned that a nearby jam factory had failed we investigated the possibility of taking over their premises. The buildings were unsuited to foundry work, but we thought we could convert them to housing. The failed factory had various trade debts, plus its ongoing responsibility to maintain 60 permanent workers. We offered to rent the factory for a sum sufficient both to service the debts and to make the monthly payment to the ex-workers. We even offered to set aside one building where the 60 workers could continue to live. Eventually, we even offered them jobs as contract workers (but not as permanent employees) in the foundry. It was no deal. The government insisted that if we really wanted the property we would also have to accept the transfer of the 60 permanent workers. Otherwise, everyone agreed, the best solution was to leave the 60 families in the empty factory. The state would pay their monthly costs and hope that something would turn up. So far nothing has.

With the labour market in a state of flux these last few years the new graduate is in a difficult position. On the one hand, the traditional system is still going strong. At the end of each school and university year the headmaster and the Labour Bureau between them cook up a work assignment (a lifetime work assignment) for each school-leaver who is not going on for further training. The cooking process depends in large part on an unwritten obligation for work units to accept the children of their employees. Most school-leavers are peasants, and in the villages the obligation is almost iron clad. A peasant youth might opt to make a life in his uncle's village rather than his father's, but he can't just turn up in any village without a connection. And peasants are barred from the towns by law. Central planning depends for its survival on the basic postulate that there is always room for a few more peasant labourers in every village. (This basic postulate is, of course, hogwash. China now has less than a quarter of a hectare of arable land for each rural labourer. Even using traditional techniques a peasant should be able to tend up to a hectare.)

The newly minted bookkeeper, pipe-fitter or draftsman has a more difficult choice. He must at least consider listening to the siren song of the new and definitely untraditional free employment market. These people and other technicians are in demand in the new private sector. The Employment Bureau (the Labour

Bureau for skilled workers) deals only in lifetime employment, so it doesn't serve joint ventures or other private-sector firms. They assemble their workforces by a mysterious process known as recruiting, which seems to many uncomfortably akin to prostitution. It offers big financial rewards, but the pool of potential recruits seems full of unsavoury characters—runaway peasants, frustrated opera singers and molesters of factory directors' daughters, to suggest just a few.

Mr So had never heard of recruiting until he met me. The foundry was often in need of production employees, but each foreman generated his own recruits. The foreman could always select one of his staff who hailed from a village in the neighbouring and impoverished province of Guangxi and send him home for a few days with enough cash to buy a few bus tickets. Each new recruit gets 30 days of training bonus while he learns the work. That's enough time to decide whether he will be able to earn a good living on piecerate, or whether he should pack it in and return home. When the foundry needed a skilled employee (a draftsman, say, or a truck driver) Mr So had only to apply to the Employment Bureau. Though it might not have any suitable candidates on its books, those in charge always knew where some were waiting in various jam factories. So recruiting in the normal sense had no place in Mr So's job description.

The village tom-tom system has always worked well, and as a joint venture Gold Land still uses it. But finding skilled staff can now be more of a problem, though it shouldn't be. We pay the highest wages for hundreds of kilometres around, our managers get occasional trips to Hong Kong, we're winning awards and surpassing targets. But in order to maintain control we refuse to use the Employment Bureau. We recruit from the rootless twilight world of the free labour market and offer only three- or five-year employment contracts. Worse yet, our employment contract has a 90-day trial period at the beginning. During that time either side can say, 'Sorry, it's not working out. Let's call it off,' and the new recruit is cast adrift in the unknown waters of unofficial unemployment. These fears are compelling, but in fact they're groundless. During 1988 and 1989 a newly trained bookkeeper, draftsman or almost anyone literate could sneak into the special economic zones at Shenzhen or Zhuhai and find a job within hours.

The first time we had to recruit an accountant I quickly discovered that I was going to have to do it personally. The school year for such people ends in July, so in March or April I discussed our needs with Mr So and asked him to drum up a few candidates for Mr Ho Hak, the Accounting Manager, to consider. He must have found this a very strange request, but in his obliging way he didn't let on. Time passed, and by June we still had no candidates. It was getting late, so I made a few enquiries and found that the whole project was way off the rails. Mr So had gone first to the Employment Bureau and been told, as he well knew, that they handle only permanent workers. He then began applying all his energies to overcoming this obstacle by the usual Chinese technique of offering the officials at the Employment Bureau various enticements while pressuring them through the government, the party and probably through someone's wife's cousin. These efforts were not entirely unsuccessful, as the bureau had promised that if, at the conclusion of their end-of-term assignment process, they had any accountants left over whom they couldn't assign they would certainly send one over to see us.

To get things moving again I got a list of the accounting schools in the area from Mr Ho and made up what Chinese businessmen like to call a 'striking force'. I rounded up a young ex-teacher, himself working for us on contract, and I explained to him and to Mr So that recruiting consisted of visiting schools, inviting students for tea, singing the praises of Gold Land and trying to assess through interviews and discussion which candidates would be worth inviting on an all-expenses-paid weekend at the factory to meet the accounting staff. Armed with some Gold Land sales brochures and the list of schools they set off in a company truck.

I'm glad I sent the young contract employee, as Mr So still didn't quite have the idea. At the first school he went straight to the Director's office, handed out some cigarettes, invited him for a meal and hammered out a deal whereby he would send us one of his best students. The new graduate would work on contract,

59

but we would have no choice. If we (or the student) were unhappy, we would be stuck until the end of the contract.

After I'd wriggled out of that agreement we finally got organised, and the young ex-teacher found us some accountant candidates in something like the conventional Western way. Mr So saw how it was done and now agrees that an old dog can be taught new tricks. (He's about 35.) But there's one more chapter to the story. After our new accountant was hired and on the job the Gaozhou Employment Bureau did in fact send around a young lady who was unhappy with the unit where she had been assigned as a bookkeeper. We hired her, too, and she turned out to be a reasonable accountant, but also a dynamite basketball player. Sometimes the old ways are best.

If you can imagine yourself in the place of one of these new graduates you can appreciate that one serious problem in any centrally planned labour market is the lack of motivators. No one has a career path; no one has anything to look forward to. Before the formation of Gold Land the old foundry had no organisation chart. The closest approximation was a list of the 30 or 40 individuals whose jobs carried some special title. But having a title was by no means an indicator of having responsibility. The workforce includes five college graduates and three secondary-school graduates. These people all had job titles, though three of the college graduates worked at the lowest level of the Engineering Department, supervising no one and with no decision-making authority. Some of the other job-title holders held the rank of Party Secretary awarded by the Communist Party. This should in principle be an entirely separate matter from their actual work assignment. A party secretary can, in principle, work as a floor sweeper. But as a courtesy these people were given the company title of Party Secretary, even though this title reflected no special company authority or responsibility.

In any case, these titles were not arranged into any kind of chart. The reason is, of course, that the old foundry had been working under the contract responsibility system and Mr Chow, feeling acutely his personal responsibility, kept all significant decision-making authority in his own hands. So the lack of an organisation chart in fact reflected the true situation. All the job titles were strictly honorary.

When we started the joint venture one of my first problems was to reverse this situation and install a Western-style organisation. I did it primarily to harness the knowledge of the existing managers and to focus each one's efforts on a particular set of responsibilities; but at the same time, the creation of a hierarchy provided a new motivator for all the employees. The new management positions have created for everyone the possibility of a career path with progression to more challenging work and better pay.

Having never known delegation the managers at first didn't understand what I was explaining, or simply disbelieved what they were hearing. We had long meetings drawing up the new organisation chart, but almost all the discussion was about the names of the departments. People weren't using the names as descriptors of the duties; they were worried about 'Quality Control and Engineering' as opposed to 'Engineering and Quality Control'. They were later surprised to discover that I intended to allow the Quality Control Manager to reject bad-quality product. But at the time they saw the organisation chart as a roll of honour with no particular functional significance.

This lack of career paths relieves a Chinese personnel manager of one of the major job responsibilities of his Western counterpart. On the other hand, lifetime employment and the low level of general education give him plenty to do on the training front. China hasn't developed an apprenticeship system on the Swiss model, nor a continuing education industry as in the United States. Nevertheless, adult education seems to be better organised than most other systems in Chinese industry. At any given time our factory has four or five promising employees away from Gaozhou taking full-time, job-related courses at universities and technical institutes. These are highly practical courses such as foundry practice, chemical analysis or accounting. Courses normally range from six months to two years in length, with the company paying all expenses and maintaining the employees' full earnings. There is no risk that the trainees will run off to work for a competitor, so the company has the employee's whole lifetime to earn a return on its investment. These courses are one of the few motivators in Chinese industry and one positive aspect of the lifetime employment system.

Mr So also organises in-house courses. One result of the no-hierarchy tradition is that these courses are open to all. They're held in the evening, usually in six or eight weekly sessions, so the employees come on their own time. I attended one course soon after the start of the joint venture and wondered why they bothered. One of our old party stalwarts stood in front of the class reading out a lecture he had written many years before and delivered many times. It was ostensibly about leadership and foremanship, but the valid points were buried in communist rhetoric and lost among the patriotic exhortations to build the motherland. If Chinese television were any better, his only students would have been applicants for party membership trying to appear keen.

But this dismal state was simply a reflection of the lack of resources. I subsequently arranged to bring in a professor of engineering from Shanghai for a series of talks on industrial engineering and workshop organisation, and the response was very enthusiastic. Our old cadre took the lead in organising things and administering the professor's end-of-course exam. Everyone praised the course, and I even saw some foremen trying to apply the professor's ideas.

The latest training innovation is the television university. As more Chinese have access to TV sets these courses are becoming popular. There are mail-order texts, and a mail-order exam is invigilated at a local school. Mr Go is taking a management course, and occasional specialised courses such as Foreign Joint Venture Legislation are appropriate. So training is one of the bright spots of Chinese industry. If only there weren't so much of it to do.

The Personnel Manager is one of the few managers in a Chinese factory with a job his Western counterpart might enjoy. Labour relations don't trouble him. The union supports and assists him. And as the final executor of the central planning of labour he has real potential to nurture a workforce and improve the lives of its members. For a man like Mr So, it's a satisfying life's work.

4

At the sharp end

WHILE Mr So can enjoy many of the job satisfactions of his Western counterpart, the Manufacturing Manager is not so lucky. His life is nothing but frustration.

The amiable Mr Go Gwong Hang, my Assistant General Manager, doubles as Gold Land's Manufacturing Manager. Mr Go is in his mid-forties, but he retains the air of what the Cantonese refer to as a *leng jai*—a handsome young man. In a special Chinese way, Mr Go has had an easy life. He is a technical-school graduate who has spent his entire career in the foundry, working his way up from the pattern shop. He had an easy Cultural Revolution, serving as the recorder at the foundry's kangaroo courts—'I was the one who wrote everything down.' Mr Go was once on the county basketball team, and the three revolutionary years when all production was at a standstill gave him plenty of time to shoot hoop.

These days, life has caught up with Mr Go. Bursitis has relegated him to coaching the company team. He's worried about getting his son through college and finding husbands for his daughters. But most of all, he's worried about working with me. Being my assistant makes Mr Go the interface between the rest of the factory and my incomprehensible Western ideas. When the other managers feel puzzled or threatened by changes they often turn to Mr Go to enquire or to complain. But Mr Go feels no more confident than they do. It puts him under a lot of pressure, and his response is to spend as little time as possible in our office's perpetual meeting. He spends his days wandering in the factory where he's more confident that he can improvise solutions to the problems that arise.

Part of Mr Go's bewilderment stems from the fact that he has spent his entire career in an enterprise with only one objective: to produce faster. The Gaozhou Foundry's overriding goal has always been to surpass its planning targets, and to surpass them as early in the year as possible. Now the joint venture has come along and imposed a quite different emphasis: meeting a particular production schedule while maintaining quality. Mr Go can now specify in advance how fast the factory will run. It is he who tells the salesmen when each order can be shipped. But he must then keep the individual promise he has made on each order. This is a new and very different assignment. At the same time, there is a new emphasis on quality. The Hong Kong salesmen are now his business partners, and they feel betrayed when a poor-quality shipment causes them trouble with their customers. From Mr Go's point of view, quality complaints have been brought into the family. It was so much simpler in the Gaozhou Foundry days.

In the early 1950s China began to follow the example of the Soviet Union in striving for self-sufficiency. With China's exploding population, the emphasis on maximising output seemed acceptable in the context of that national objective. Then, in the early 1980s, there was a change of national strategy. The government was faced with Hong Kong and Japanese joint-venture proposals that would provide employment and earn foreign exchange for China as a supplier of low-technology manufactured goods to the world. In the case of the Hong Kong proposals the businessmen behind them were often motivated in part by a sincere patriotic desire to help China to develop, as well as by commercial concerns.

Acceptance of this assistance involved suspending many of the key mechanisms of central planning, so this ideological apostasy was explained by referring to the changes as 'modernisations'. The new policy was christened the 'Four Modernisations' campaign, and its explicit aim was to improve the efficiency of agriculture, industry, science and technology, and the armed forces by applying Western methods. Foreign businesses were invited to help, and a framework was created to encourage joint ventures between Chinese state enterprises and private firms from overseas.

The rules which evolved in the 1980s to regulate these new joint ventures assumed that modern technology was to be a major contribution of the foreign partner. But it didn't take long to discover that the modernisation of industry was as much a question of management methods as of production equipment. Furthermore, the methods that were obviously required quickly proved to be incompatible with central planning. So by the late 1980s it was clear that the 'Four Modernisations' were not going to be the salvation of scientific socialism. In every sector, joint ventures that had been licensed to operate outside socialist principles were not only outperforming their state counterparts, but were also delivering better welfare for their employees.

By 1988 it was officially accepted that China would develop and exploit a comparative advantage in low-technology manufactured goods such as toys and clothing. These are the items which powered Hong Kong's economic development, and the patriotic Hong Kong entrepreneurs were then, as now, anxious to develop less expensive sources of supply in order to maintain their positions in the world market in the face of increasing competition. Hong Kong traders proposed that if China could learn from them how to manufacture these items to international standards, the traders could manage the overseas marketing. China could earn substantial foreign exchange, which could then be applied to importing modern technology to upgrade power generation, communications and the rest of China's infrastructure.

Cast iron is a rather old-fashioned material which is used these days primarily in applications which call for a large mass of low-performance metal. Manhole covers are a familiar example. They wear well, they don't move when traffic rolls over them, and they're too heavy for vandals to tamper with. Many sorts of brake shoes and brake drums are cast in iron to absorb heat without deforming. In the home, cast iron skillets heat evenly, and stoves and furnaces often have many cast iron parts. Other materials could do these jobs, but cast iron is cheaper.

In most countries iron foundries are being driven out of business by difficulties in recruiting labour and minimising pollution, but this simply opens the door for China. China has pervasive underemployment and a fast-growing population. Casting iron may be hot and dirty work, but for a Gaozhou peasant the alternative is walking behind a water buffalo knee deep in muck. For the time being, coal is China's only available fuel for most cooking and heating, so air pollution is a fact of life. On the other hand, China can make cast iron using only domestic materials. Most other exports, even clothing, depend on importing some of the materials for assembly, and these imports eat away at the foreign exchange earnings. All of this is clear to the economic czars in Beijing. If foreign countries are willing to let China supply their manhole covers, the planners can see the wisdom of committing some of their iron-casting capacity to serving this demand and earning foreign exchange.

Through most of Mr Go's career the Gaozhou Foundry had three types of markets. The biggest and in every way the most important was to deliver to the state under the central plan. A second outlet was to sell for export through one of the state import/export agencies. Then there was the possibility of selling on the private domestic market (although in cast iron products this market is rather limited). Growth in output normally came through deliveries to the state, with export orders as icing on the top. This put the pressure squarely on manufacturing.

In the Gaozhou Foundry days this pressure didn't land directly on Mr Go. It was Mr Chow, then the Factory Director, who had the personal responsibility contract, so Mr Chow was inclined to apply much of his energy to personally expediting production. In the joint venture the General Manager stands in the place of the conventional Factory Director. But one of my objectives as General Manager is to introduce delegation into the organisation. So I insist that Mr Go take primary responsibility for quality and schedules. Understandably, he feels a bit exploited.

In a state-owned work unit planning targets are set annually in negotiations between the Factory Director and the bureau supervising his responsibility contract. For most foundries this bureau will be the local Economic Committee. The targets originate from the national Five-year Plan, but any trace of that framework is lost by the time talks get to the work-unit level. As in most enterprises in any country, planning starts from the current year's results. The Factory Director's objective is to negotiate a plan target bigger than last year's and then to exceed it. Three years of that and he'll have cash for a new motorcycle plus renewal of his contract. The local Economic Committee has nominally the same goals, but as bureaucrats they're risk-averse. They have little interest in a bigger target for a particular work unit, but they certainly don't want to end the year having to explain a shortfall to the regional authorities. Worse yet, bigger targets mean that they have to round up a bigger raw material allocation. If the factory fails to use all of it, the numbers in the regional reports will show waste of raw materials in their town. So the Economic Committee is inclined to caution.

Once the annual target has been agreed there is remarkably loose control. The Gaozhou Foundry, for example, used to be assigned to cast thousands of wheel hubs for the carts that are used to convey merchandise throughout China. It was just one of many, many foundries supplying the total national demand for this item. The weekly demand depends on all sorts of materials, electricity and transport problems at the cart factories. They too may make other products and may not make carts at a steady rate all year round. The foundry had no idea what was happening at the particular cart factory that was getting its hubs, nor how things were going with the other suppliers.

At Gold Land we still make hubs as a bit of a sideline, but fortunately we don't have to rely on them. We never know when a truck will turn up looking for hubs. They have no set order; they just take what we have and leave us to get on with making more. It seems to work a bit like automatic delivery of home heating oil. The cart maker knows how fast his suppliers can produce, so when he needs hubs he can estimate pretty closely how many have accumulated at each foundry since he last cleaned them out, and he sends out trucks accordingly.

In this situation the ambitious Factory Director of a state-owned work unit has only one rational course of action: take whatever planning targets he has been given and begin producing as fast as possible. If the goods pile up rusting in the yard that's not his problem. If the surface is a bit rough and the paint job pretty thin, that doesn't bother him either, as long as these points are not specifically mentioned in the quality specifications. If there are hidden defects in the castings even that is not too troublesome, as long as they don't fail until after they've been mixed in with the castings from all the other suppliers. The defects cannot then be deducted back from his foundry's output figures.

So don't waste time worrying about the cart factory's requirements. Full speed ahead. Because the only sure way to get a target increase is to finish this year's target in October or November. The Economic Committee too must boost output and employment, so a factory that completes its target puts the onus on them to come up with more quota for the balance of the year. Normally this is readily available in the unfilled quotas of other units. So manufacturing is the department which can earn the director his bonus; as a result, it's under incessant pressure. Corporate strategy is reduced to producing as much as possible, as quickly as possible:

When the strategic planners in Beijing had only these state units to rely on, it's clear why they had difficulty mandating export-led growth. Exporting is troublesome to factory directors because it requires more careful attention to quality and because the exporters impose strict shipping schedules. One major success of the 'Four Modernisations' has been the discovery that joint ventures are far more effective than the system of import/export agencies in encouraging factories to take exporting seriously. China does have a comparative advantage in certain types of manufactured goods, and once a Chinese factory has learned to understand the attitudes and requirements of foreign customers it has access to an enormous market which can fulfil the Factory Director's four targets even better than producing for the plan.

During our first year Gold Land shipped almost two-and-a-half times the output of the foundry in its last year before the joint venture, and profits were ten times the foundry's previous figure. Naturally, employment increased and the employees took home much bigger piecework payments. In addition, the foreign partner put in some capital investment. So Mr Chow, who is still the contract holder for the old foundry, had all his hopes fulfilled.

As his replacement I have the different problem of trying to re-educate every part of the organisation in the objectives and attitudes of the foreign customers. These lessons touch every department, but the two most important lessons, and the most urgent, have been about maintaining quality and about shipping on the customer's schedule rather than at our own convenience. The primary target for these key lessons has been the Manufacturing Department, so Mr Go has been under the gun.

Before I took over at Gold Land, I studied the records in Hong Kong and found it hard to imagine how the old foundry's delivery record could be so bad. It was difficult to find any order for anything which had ever been shipped on time. Every customer's file contained long telex exchanges enquiring, threatening and finally pleading on the single subject of 'Where are the castings?'. Large orders with shipments scheduled over several months were quite often partially cancelled. Items like barbecue grilles are strongly seasonal, and after a certain date the customers in Europe would simply cancel anything not yet shipped. The foundry rarely completed more than 80 per cent of these big orders before the customer lost patience. I recall one major item where only 15 per cent of the total quantity had been completed before the customer had to cancel the rest. It seemed obvious that with no additional sales effort Gold Land could easily surpass the foundry's previous annual output by simply completing all the work in the order book before the deadlines.

In my first weeks at Gold Land I had to untangle an order that was about six months late. The product was still stuck in the factory when it should already have been on display in the stores in the United States. It was a problem of nuts—the product was screwed together on a threaded rod and fastened with a pair of them. Because it was being sold in the United States it required nuts with American-specification threads. China is (to a certain extent) on the metric system, so such nuts are hard to buy in

China and had been ordered from Hong Kong. The factory had been running on short lead times, and the original order for nuts had been placed too late; so no nuts were on hand to assemble the first production. When they did finally arrive the threads were correct, but the nuts were the wrong colour, and they were too thick to fit into the product. So the whole lot had to be reordered. Elsewhere, in such an emergency, a manufacturing manager would appoint an expediter, give him a plane ticket and tell him to solve the problem. But an expediter with a good political record would need eight months to get a visa to leave China, so expediting was limited to repeated phone calls and cables.

Once I was installed in Gaozhou I saw the other side of these sad stories. The Hong Kong distributor had been feeding the factory one order at a time. Hong Kong took the view that encouraging the foundry to dabble in forward planning would only divert attention from the ever-present urgently late orders. So the foundry had been running with no order backlog. Every production run had ended with either a furious rush shipment or a sudden cancellation. In either case, the management was left with employees paid on piecework and no work to give them. Their first response was to book a telephone call to Hong Kong and try to find out what was coming next. (While waiting to get through they must have often contemplated the advantages of manufacturing for the state instead of for export.) But until the specifications for the new product had been worked out they needed to give the employees something to do. So, believe it or not, they carried on with the just-completed item.

When I first realised this was going on I was staggered. I'd never seen such a thing. The factory was full of little piles of rusty left-overs made on the end of previous contracts and awaiting the day when that item might be ordered again. Worse yet, under the old foundry's accounting system, all that production had been credited against the foundry's annual output target and solemnly entered into the inventory. If it were fed back to the furnaces and melted down into new product the difference between its inventory value and its scrap value would be charged to Mr Chow personally as 'waste'. Much of this old stuff was completely obsolete, as the designs had been changed in subsequent years or the product discontinued.

Some of the inventory stayed with us for more than a year, but we were able to get the deliveries back on schedule in only a few months. It was a good example of how the presence of a foreigner was enough in itself to enable us to slice through a long-standing Gordian knot. Order backlog and production scheduling systems had existed for the managers of the foundry only as concepts in books. I had worked with them before, and with the benefit of practical experience it wasn't difficult to design something and get it running. I also had the advantage of being able to travel to Hong Kong, sit down with the sales people and explain the backlog problem in terms they could understand. In doing so I discovered that none of the Hong Kong staff had any manufacturing experience. So we roughed out a capacity measure for the company, laid out all the orders and all the 'possibles' and 'probables' on a twelve-month forward plan, and set up a few guidelines on lead time from placing an order to the first shipment. This is absolutely basic stuff to any Western factory, but in Gaozhou it was a revelation. It took Mr Go and Ah Bo, the Purchasing Manager, about ten seconds to see how this was going to make things a lot easier, though they couldn't really believe that Hong Kong as the customer would actually go out of its way to help them in this way. These are not the kinds of things that the 'Four Modernisations' campaign was originally intended to modernise, but this is where the policy has had its biggest and most beneficial impact. I was ashamed to take the credit for solving such a major problem so easily.

The quality problem was by no means such a cinch. The files I had read in Hong Kong had turned up some pretty ghastly tales. Eighty per cent of the correspondence in the files was about late deliveries, but most of the rest consisted of quality complaints. There were whole containers of rusty product, thousands of broken cartons, design problems, dirty product—every sort of serious fault. But the most memorable file included photographs from Germany of whole containers full of mould. Apparently the product had been packed wet, and during the two-month journey to Europe all the cartons had disintegrated into a mouldy mass. They had difficulty in Germany finding employees

71

willing to help empty the container on to the scrap heap. And this had happened more than once. What could be going on?

This time the explanation was a lot more complex, but there were two factors at the root of it all. First, the prices for most of the products had not been adjusted very much for several years. Prices in China are 'set' by a bureaucrat, not determined by supply and demand, and the prices for these products had not kept up with China's very substantial inflation during the 1980s. This was exacerbated by the same problem of short lead times that had been causing the delivery problems. In an effort to hold down the price the foundry was turning to the cheapest sources for cartons. The cheapest carton supplier in the Gaozhou area was, in fact, a small private enterprise. The Director, Mr So, introduced me to the realities of carton making in China.

Mr So's factory consisted of two disused warehouses facing each other across a narrow dirt lane on the slopes of a hillside topped by an old and impressive pagoda. These modest premises housed equipment even more modest. His employees cranked by hand a set of rollers similar to the wringer on an old-fashioned washing-machine. One of the pair of rollers was ribbed, so when wet paper was put through the wringer it emerged corrugated to form the rippled inner layer of a sheet of carton material. This was brushed with glue on each side and faced with smooth paper to make the final cardboard sheet. It was an essential part of Mr So's process that the cardboard sheets should then be cut and stapled into freestanding box form and immediately placed out in the road to dry in the sun.

'Mr So,' I asked, 'what do you do when it rains?' Mr So had apparently been afraid I would ask that question. 'The rainy season is a problem for us,' he replied. And with some resignation he ushered me into a room he had constructed at the end of one of the buildings. The ceiling was covered with 40-watt light bulbs. Arrayed on the floor were perhaps a dozen small electric heaters. A wire gridwork was installed about 50 cm off the floor, and on this the cartons were erected with the top and bottom open to be dried by the heaters and the light bulbs. A nice try; too bad it didn't work.

China is not short of people, and it's no longer short of food. It could use more arable land, and some places are badly short of water, but what is really in short supply in China is fuel. As an alternative to burning coal Chinese peasants would prefer to send some of their surplus labour out to cut wood for free fuel, so the government has found it necessary to strictly control all uses of wood so as to prevent the countryside being stripped bare. As a result of these controls, paper, particularly in south China, is normally made not from wood but from grass and straw. Good, international-quality cartons are sometimes obtainable in China, but the cost is much higher because the quality can be maintained only by making them from imported pulp or paper.

These expensive cartons were not, of course, what the foundry had been specifying; and in any case these high-quality cartons were not Mr So's line of business. As a small rural work unit he would have had virtually insurmountable difficulties trying to import paper. So Mr So's cartons were made from grass. Beyond being made from grass, they were pulped with chemicals which left the resulting paper slightly hygroscopic. Even after drying they would re-absorb water and turn soft just standing around in the humid Gaozhou heat. Like fresh pasta, it was best to use Mr So's cartons within a few days. Not really the thing for shipping to Europe.

I'm sad to admit that Mr So has been one of the casualties of the 'Four Modernisations'. Gold Land now buys its cartons from a larger and more expensive supplier—whom we still suspect of slipping some grass paper into the goods, but who at least owns a drying oven.

Cartons were just one aspect of the quality problem, but most of the foundry's quality disasters had stories like the carton saga behind them.

Gaozhou is not on the rail line, and the sandy river that flows through town is too shallow for barges, so export products must be trucked over 425 km of potholed roads to the port at Guangzhou. Many units operate their own trucks for this sort of work, but the foundry made a practice of hiring trucks from other units or from private operators on a trip-by-trip basis. The design of these trucks seems to be an unmodified copy of American trucks left behind after the Second World War. Many still

73

have the headlights on little posts on top of the front fenders. They have running boards, and for ventilation the whole front windshield is hinged to tip out. The design is sometimes called a stake truck: the bed at the back has slatted sides and a tailgate, and the top is open, perhaps with hoops across for a canvas cover. The bed measures 2 by 5 metres with a nominal capacity of 5 tonnes.

You hire one of these trucks by the tonne-kilometre. For several years Mr Chow had resisted any increase in the fee per tonne-kilometre, so despite the relatively high value of our products we were paying less than most other units for our trucking. We got away with it because cast iron has a very high density. The operators were willing to serve us at these low rates only if they controlled the loading, as they had developed techniques for loading up to 12 tonnes on one of these 5-tonne trucks. The techniques involved shoehorning cartons of product into every cubic centimetre of the truck's capacity, and then squeezing in a few more cartons where none seemed possible. It earned the driver a decent return for his trip, and it assured us of cheap trucking. The problem is that it destroyed the cartons.

Rather than sitting squarely, interlocked to support each other, some cartons were shoehorned in at odd angles. They then bounced on edge through their twelve-hour trip to Guangzhou. The cartons were a bit damp and soft to begin with, and the canvas covering offered only partial protection against rain and dust along the way. It was pretty clear why the product was reaching Guangzhou looking as if it had just survived the siege of Stalingrad. I can imagine that the famous mould set in when a truck hit a particularly heavy rainstorm on the way to Guangzhou and arrived with the cartons thoroughly wet. The warehouse employees in Guangzhou were not foundry employees; they worked for the state import/export agency which handled the foundry's exports. They had no interest in trying to dry out or repack the product, and in any case no means to do so. Their response was to get the sodden cartons into a container, seal it up and pass the problem on to some other work unit. In this case, the 'other work unit' was the German customer.

So the major quality problems had a number of interlocking

causes. It took a few weeks to figure out all the pieces of the puzzle, and then many months to sort out a set of solutions and get them implemented. A year and a half later we were shipping on pallets, each pallet wrapped in plastic film to protect against dust. But it was a long road to travel step by step.

There are no pallets for sale in Gaozhou. Indeed, no one in the foundry had ever worked with them. We eventually located a subcontractor who could manufacture pallets for us, but only after I had personally drawn one from memory and exhaustively explained what it was and how it could be helpful. It wasn't that easy to explain. If you've worked in a foundry all your life and never seen a pallet it doesn't seem on first consideration to be much of an idea. A pallet is heavy. You need special equipment to move it around. They break and have to be repaired or replaced. And in China, made from wood, they're reasonably expensive. Then too, if you're the only work unit using pallets, you also need a system to ensure that your pallets come back to you. In our case, we need to run truckloads of empty pallets back from Guangzhou every week or two. The big inventory of idle pallets takes up space. And even if they're a pretty crazy idea for moving goods they could make dandy chicken coops, so you have to keep them away from sticky-fingered employees. As the pallet pioneer I spent a lot of time and effort wading backwards and forwards through the rice paddy of these arguments. In the end I probably prevailed with such a silly proposal only on the strength of my status as an experienced foreigner.

We eventually manufactured some pallets. We found a hand truck for sale in Guangzhou. We built a loading dock and reorganised our system for loading trucks. But even then we weren't home free. Poking around the factory one night I discovered ten or fifteen pallet loads that stood packed, waiting for shipping, but with the cartons stacked in separate piles on the pallets like so many decks of cards. Anyone trying to move the pallet would find, especially with our soft and bulging cartons, that the stacks would tend to collapse and scatter burst cartons all over the floor.

'We were wondering about that,' Mr Go said the next day. 'But come on,' I said. 'You wouldn't build a brick wall without interlocking the bricks.' (You can say that sort of thing to people in

China, where if you want something built you have no option but to build it yourself.) 'Well, yes,' said Mr Go. 'But you do that by cutting half a brick to start the second row.' So after everything else I sat down and designed some patterns for interlocking the stacks of cartons on the pallets. Our palletised shipping is working now, but getting there was hard wading every step of the way.

In the case of the pallets we persisted in introducing new technology because the old methods were delivering unsaleable rubbish. With many other modernisation proposals the case for change is not so clear. For example, the typical Chinese factory has little in the way of labour-saving equipment. Old ladies push heavy castings around in wheelbarrows, and hundreds of parts are piled on the floor to be processed or moved one by one. But in the context of central planning this is not unreasonable. For the central planner, labour is in surplus and is a fixed cost. Whatever the workers do they must be fed. In the unlikely event that all the workers could ever be fully employed there is still a vast army of under-employed peasants. With labour in surplus, labour saving for its own sake is not on the agenda.

The standard of education of our permanent workforce is a problem that resists all wizardry. Before Gold Land was founded the foundry had run for many years without ever doing a proper check on the inventory. The lack of numerate manpower helps to explain why the foundry didn't have much of a tradition of inventory verification, but it's also true that under the contract responsibility system any shortages noted at inventory time would have caused trouble for Mr Chow. So with no auditors to complain there had always been a tendency to use the book values uncorrected year after year. If there were supposed to be 1000 widgets in a pile in the back lot covered with weeds, call it 1000 until the day someone orders them. Then if it turns out there were only 900 all along, one of the workshops can run off the extra 100 and hide it in the accounts. At Gold Land I don't have to take personal responsibility for every shortage, so we've tried to be a bit more precise.

Thus it was that at the time of our first inventory check the perpetual meeting in my office was taken over for a while by an argument about shovels. Not how many we owned, but how many we would have to buy to check our stock of coke. We normally keep hundreds of tonnes of the stuff, so at first I couldn't understand what they could be arguing about. (Well, at the very first I couldn't understand because I didn't know the Cantonese name for a shovel.) Eventually I realised that Mr Ho Hak, our Accounting Manager, actually intended to count everything in the foundry. He was going to move our entire stock of coke from one side of the coke yard to the other, and weigh it on the way.

I went to see Mr Ho, and we had a lengthy chat. He's one of our few high-school graduates—literate, reasonably numerate, a dab hand at the abacus, and a hard-working, serious bookkeeper. But he had never in his life studied statistics. As far as he was concerned, if you had 1000 tonnes of pig iron in the form of 50 000 pigs of 20 kg each, the only way to inventory it was to count every pig. And if the 20 kg wasn't reliable, you had to weigh each one as well. Hmmm.

'Here's a suggestion,' I said, trying to be helpful. 'All the iron in the yard arrived in just four or five big shipments. Why don't you weigh ten or fifteen pigs from each shipment and calculate an average weight? Then you can simply count the pigs in one small area and use that number to figure out the number of pigs in the whole yard. Multiply by the average weight, and you can calculate the whole stock in a couple of hours with only two men.' (He'd asked for 25.) 'But it would be wrong,' he pointed out, reasonably enough. Well, strictly speaking, yes it would be. 'Don't worry. This is how it's done in Western countries.' 'Ah,' he said, 'but this is China.' (A very common rejoinder in these situations.) 'The auditors from Guangzhou would never stand for it.'

What could I do? In his uncertainty and insecurity he was standing on his professional integrity. I checked with our Quality Control Manager and found that she at least, a university graduate, had a working knowledge of sampling and statistical inference. I enlisted her help to try and spread a little understanding through the rest of the management. But our inventories still seem to involve a lot of unnecessary work.

When people say that a developing country has a poor infrastructure they usually mean there are power cuts and the phones don't work. But down on the casting floor our infrastructure problems are even more basic. Many of our products are composed primarily of cast iron but have various smaller parts of other materials. A cast iron barbecue, for example, may have a wire grille on the top made from electroplated steel wire. The handles may be of wood and the legs of rolled sheet metal. We subcontract all of these non-cast parts to other factories around the Gaozhou area. Often these are small, one-family operations and Gold Land is their biggest customer. We try to maintain a steady flow of work to keep these small firms in business, or we would be continually searching for and training new subcontractors. As private sector firms these suppliers are in constant danger of being shut down by the government simply as deviations from socialism. (After the Tiananmen massacre of June 1989 there was just such a crackdown, but it had lost much of its militancy by the time the proclamations reached Gaozhou and our subcontractors all escaped.) When the foundry had no future planning of its orders, keeping these subcontractors working was complicated and sometimes impossible, but Gold Land's new longer-range order book has made this problem somewhat less acute.

Some subcontracting, however, cannot be done locally. If we need hot dip galvanising, for example, the only supplier is at least a day away by truck, half a day by telephone and a week by mail. In this case we are not the galvaniser's largest customer, so we must accept our share of all his production delays. And as a state work unit he has plenty.

Just sending parts for processing can be difficult. There is no system of common carriers with an agreed tariff. We have to negotiate with one of our independent truckers to make a special trip. Normally he won't be anxious to go; and unless the subcontractor is located in a major city he certainly won't go for the usual rate per tonne-kilometre, because in a small city where he has no relationships the trucker is not likely to find a load to come back. So he'll want an extra payment, specially negotiated trip by trip, to compensate him for the risk of running empty. Of course, the ideal arrangement would be to send one lot of parts for processing and ask the truck to bring back the last lot. But with unreliable communications, the subcontractor's unstable electricity supply and a dozen other factors, it never quite works out that way.

In any case, trucks are in such short supply that for a given two- or three-day period it might be difficult to find a truck available to make the trip. We ship one or two truckloads of product to Guangzhou every night, but late in the afternoon you'll sometimes find our Shipping Manager pedalling around town looking for an available truck because the vehicle he had expected didn't turn up to load. At holidays, and especially in the two or three weeks leading up to the important lunar New Year celebrations, truckers usually raise their rates temporarily to earn some extra money and to compensate for the time away from home during the holiday season. When all these problems have been resolved, there is sometimes difficulty finding enough fuel for the trip.

Subcontracting and trucking are just two general examples of the infrastructural problems a Manufacturing Manager in China expects to handle in trying to keep the factory running and co-ordinated. The possible foul-ups are endless. You might expect that once a proper order book was in operation these problems would be reduced considerably. Unfortunately, there is a deeper co-ordination problem which in most cases seems to be exacerbated, not relieved, by the efforts of a foreign partner. What usually does it is a decision by the foreign partner to install some new equipment. The problem with new equipment is that production in a whole range of Chinese factories is, as much as they can make it, a batch process. This allows the different departments to work independently with a minimum of formal co-ordination. The foreign partner, on the other hand, wants to bring in a modern machine which often is either a continuous-flow operation or which requires a steady flow of the same sort of parts to keep it running efficiently. For the first time, the Chinese managers must publish and adhere to a reasonably detailed production schedule. Pandemonium ensues.

Just such a situation led to the biggest disruption we ever faced at Gold Land. We tried to insert a mechanical painting line into the long-entrenched semi-batch operations of the foundry. We have six workshops making iron castings. Two others machine the castings to final form. Another separate workshop paints, assembles and packs the final product. Each workshop had always worked to its monthly contract of various pieces to do and was paid by the piece. But the foreman was free to schedule the work within his workshop to compensate for the vicissitudes I've described and to keep all of his employees working. There had always been some co-ordination among the workshops, of course, as the pieces moved from one to another through the process. But this had been minimal. The flow was maintained primarily through the simple but rather expensive expedient of keeping a lot of partly processed work lying around between workshops. That way, if Foundry 4 didn't deliver the expected 10 000 furnace doors, the machining workshop could turn to some ash grates that had been received from Foundry 6 a few days earlier but left sitting around.

The new painting machine was a very different beast. It was a long assembly line based on a conveyor holding hundreds of parts at one time. Ostensibly it should save paint (good-quality paint is very expensive in China) and at the same time improve the appearance of the finished paint job. But from the factory's point of view its biggest impact was in revolutionising Mr Go's nastiest job: co-ordination.

Like any high-capacity machine, this one was designed to run efficiently when it's running, but changing from one product to another was wasteful and troublesome. Suddenly the whole factory had to learn to supply particular parts on a tight schedule to ensure that the painting line never stopped and that it moved smoothly from one product to another in an efficient sequence. It was particularly important, for example, to paint all the various white items before moving on to the green ones, as changing colours back and forth required hours of extra cleaning. Foremen and employees who previously had a lot of discretion in scheduling work within their monthly quota were suddenly having to work to a written daily schedule for the first time. When things went wrong, they had to expedite.

It was quite a shock to the foundry's sclerotic system. We eventually changed the work habits of the experienced foremen who had worked in the typical Chinese batch system all their lives, but it was a difficult startup. Unfortunately, the concept of modernisation makes this kind of clash of industrial cultures as frequent as it is inevitable. In a sense, it's the essence of modernisation. If China wants to play the joint-venture game there's no real alternative. But that doesn't make it fun.

Mr Go, then, is fighting to change the traditional work practices and the traditional thinking of Gold Land's workforce. Only by reorienting them towards maintaining quality and shipping on time can he meet the new higher standards of the joint-venture environment. Change always seems threatening— in totalitarian China even more than elsewhere. Mr Go has to apply a judicious mix of carrot and stick to achieve the desired results. He has fewer sanctions at his disposal than managers in a capitalist enterprise. He must rely to a much greater extent on motivating through pure exhortation. At Gold Land this problem may be more acute than in other work units because we rely so heavily on the piecerate.

In conventional Chinese factories the Factory Director uses the bonus component of each employee's pay to maintain his personal authority. The Factory Director reserves the right to adjust bonuses at will, rewarding those who please him and depriving those who don't. This has obvious problems, but the piecerate alternative, by making pay a matter of objective calculation, removes an important management tool.

In every factory there are always clean-up, rework and reorganising jobs to be done. They don't directly turn out any product; they're just one-off little clean-ups. But if they are neglected the workshop gets in a mess and it becomes harder to get the real work accomplished. Everyone realises that these things must be attended to as they arise, but under a piecework pay system no one is willing to put aside his production work for an hour or two to deal with them. The foreman has to, in effect, create a special piecerate for each of these one-off tasks. To get an employee to clean out a blocked drain the foreman must promise a one-off payment equivalent to what the employee could earn on piecework during that time.

On the other hand, paying on piecework gives us a certain flexibility. For example, winter is the dry season in Gaozhou, when the reservoirs run low and electricity is bound to be in short supply. In the autumn the Electricity Bureau and the Economic Committee arrange a winter schedule of rotating power cuts for each work unit. In 1989 we were scheduled to be without electricity on Tuesdays, Thursdays and Saturdays throughout the day. The piecerate system helps the Manufacturing Manager to adapt to this kind of inconvenience relatively easily. He can reschedule the factory for night and Sunday operations confident that the employees will co-operate fully.

Conversely, if we have a dark rainy day, the power may be on but the employees may decide to stay at home or to go home early. It might be a Wednesday, but even full power isn't enough to run both lights and fans at the same time. If it's hot the employees need the fans, but if it's dark they can't work properly. If they're making too many defective pieces because they can't see to work, many staff will quite reasonably decide to spend the day at home rather than waste their time struggling in the dark for little pay. To make up their income they'll perhaps return at night when few others are working and most of the machines are turned off.

So, while the piecework system helps us to adapt to almost any disruption, it also encourages a kind of unco-ordinated individual initiative which makes production as a whole difficult to control.

If he's put in a position of enforcing basic discipline, Mr Go has a problem. Dismissals are simply impossible. As his ultimate weapon in this direction he can go only as far as reassignment. Assigning a recalcitrant employee to toilet cleaning, for example, would be counter-productive, since it's not on piecework, and it has a small guaranteed income whether or not the toilets are cleaned. A miscreant transferred to toilet cleaning would simply apply himself to some sort of private business while collecting his basic benefits, and the toilets would remain uncleaned. Indeed, the ultimate reassignment sanction is to throw money at a malefactor—assign him to a hard, hot and dirty job in the foundry. He then must work to eat, but of course these are the jobs with the highest piecerates.

With such feeble sticks at his disposal Mr Go must rely primarily on carrots to change people's habits. The discretionary bonus carrot has been killed off by piecework pay. Tampering with the rates is not an available carrot, as it's important to keep all the rates for different jobs in rough proportion so that employees can be transferred from one kind of work to another without too much argument. Instead, to get good-quality product out the door daily, Mr Go relies heavily on pure exhortation. His principal mechanism is the weekly production meeting. It's not much to fall back on.

The production meeting, Gold Land's only regular formal meeting, convenes at 2.30 every Friday afternoon. The meeting room is arranged with rows of benches like a church; there are no tables except low tea tables for the refreshments. At the front are a desk and chair for the speaker. The meeting brings together all the foremen, the heads of the supporting departments and the general management—about 30 people in all. This may sound like a pretty big meeting, and it is; but the content suits the form.

The whole procedure has been adapted from another kind of meeting which was rare in Gold Land when we began but which became more common after the pro-democracy demonstrations in Beijing in the spring of 1989. This is the meeting to 'study documents'. It's common in many enterprises that on Saturday afternoon the party members are released from their regular duties to study the latest documents handed down through the government or the parallel party hierarchy. If there is nothing special that week, they meet anyway and read editorials from the party newspaper, the *People's Daily*. It's reasonable enough that a meeting with that agenda should begin with a reading of the documents in question. (Literacy is not a prerequisite for party membership.) The organisation's Party Secretary, who chairs the meeting, then normally starts the discussion by raising a few salient points. When the weekly management meeting convenes it follows this same programme, because this is the only format people know.

I make a point of showing up on time, but this is not really in the spirit of the occasion. It shows that I don't fully appreciate the background to this weekly ritual, which has its roots in the

Cultural Revolution and probably in Chinese opera. In a Western business meeting people with diverse knowledge and viewpoints exchange ideas to work out a plan which everyone understands and agrees to follow. These meetings at Gold Land involve almost no audience participation and no exchange of information. The audience comes to hear the speaker's comments, learn his attitudes and receive his instructions. It's Lenin's democratic centralism writ small.

The workshop managers have ample opportunity to express their views to Mr Go or to me any day, any time. They have only to break into the perpetual meeting in my office or buttonhole Mr Go on his wanderings through the factory. In these daily encounters everyone's opinion is always welcomed on every subject, debate is encouraged and views are expressed frankly and forcefully. If necessary, decisions are taken on the spot. But unlike Western procedure, these day-to-day discussions are not documented with minutes, and the decisions are not disseminated in memos. These functions are partially taken up instead by the regular Friday meeting.

Most Gold Land managers don't own a watch, and even those who do choose not to wear their watches on the casting floor, so attendees at these meetings drift in rather slowly over a period of about 15 minutes. Mr Go intentionally waits to arrive last, because the meeting starts with his arrival. This is a bit of a special arrangement. Normally I should run the meeting, so I should arrive last after Mr Go has rounded up any stragglers. In fact, when Mr Go arrives I call the meeting to order, spend perhaps 10 minutes running through any points I particularly want to announce or comment on and then I turn the meeting over to the chairman.

I open the meeting standing at my seat in the front row. Mr Go, however, moves to the front and takes the seat at the desk, because he now intends to speak for about two hours without interruption. At the beginning he has notes on two or three subjects just to get himself going, but the bulk of it is extemporaneous. He's a pretty good orator. He speaks distinctly, and at an appropriate speed and volume. He adjusts his cadence to the topic and modulates his voice to emphasise his points. But however engaging his delivery, two hours is a long time. I try not to doze off, but I'm familiar with more or less everything he's saying. The others don't share this disadvantage but feel less duty-bound to stay awake. No one reads the newspaper or plays cards as they would at the opera, but gradually conversations are begun and a low murmur fills the room. Tea is always served, so there is a certain amount of wandering about pouring and refilling the teapot. And, of course, after 45 minutes or so the tea begins to impel listeners out to the lavatory. There are one or two water-pipes being passed, so the burbling and the continual striking of matches add to the background noise.

Mr Go normally dwells on the production figures. He reports on the progress of any special projects, criticises errors and praises good work. He may announce arrangements for an upcoming event such as coverage for a holiday. In short, during this meeting he covers all the matters that would circulate around a Western office in the form of reports, announcements, memos and the company newspaper.

When he has finished Mr Go passes the floor in turn to each of the other managers. They can add their own announcements if he has missed something, but normally they comment on and refine what my assistant has said. In particular, it's interesting that anyone who has been criticised in the main address is normally expected to speak up when his turn comes. He may defend himself, but much more often he contributes a self-criticism with a plan and promise for future improvement.

About 30 per cent of this long weekly address consists of substantive points which vary from week to week. The filler, which always allows Mr Go to conclude at about 20 minutes to 5, is exhortation, woven into all the substantive topics in a seamless continuum. There are weekly references to 'our striking force', 'all-out assaults' and 'forced marches'. Mr Go is not an army veteran, but these seem to be popular metaphors for any Chinese leader in his situation.

One main objective of these meetings is to raise the 'fighting spirit' of our workforce, and this is the method. In the last analysis Mr Go is appealing to our managers, as lifelong compulsory participants in Gold Land's successes and failures, to work longer, harder and more diligently for reasons of personal, work unit and local pride—and even out of national patriotism.

As someone who will not be working at Gold Land or in China for his whole life, it's difficult for me to appreciate the strength of these appeals. I simply find Gold Land a uniquely intriguing place to work and I take personal satisfaction in seeing it work better as a result of my personal contribution. But I rarely see this kind of self-centred reasoning among my colleagues. Gold Land's success really is their success; the two are inseparable. So these weekly appeals seem to have their effect. For Gold Land's managers the weekly two hours of exhortation is the heart of the production management process.

I should mention one other carrot in Mr Go's management repertoire. He arranges annual tea-parties. Unusual as this may sound, the tea-parties are not actually a very original idea. The foundry learned about them from the Economic Committee. The committee gives each work unit in Gaozhou its annual target, and each year in late October or early November the most successful units in town begin to hit their targets for the year. The committee then organises a sort of high-level tea-party for the leaders of all the local industries to announce these successes and present the directors of the first six target-achievers with cash prizes, certificates, newspaper publicity and the applause of their peers. I've received some of these awards and I must admit that if I had lived my entire life with the others in the room it would be an effective reward for me personally.

Gold Land is usually one of the first six, and we come back from these things full of tea and bananas with a big red envelope full of money—usually 500 to 1000 yuan (a couple of hundred US dollars). The first year I asked what we should do with the money, but Mr Go assured me, 'Don't worry. We'll need all that and more for the workshop parties.' Parties?

'Well, it's the workshops who achieved the targets. Our targets are just the sum of their targets.'

'Hold on. You and I set the workshops' targets every month based on the order position. The employees and the foremen don't know anything about it.'

'That's true,' he agreed. 'But what they do know is that the foundry has always had an annual target. By the time the driver parks this truck they'll know we've been to a party. They'll be waiting for their turn.'

So having been fêted by the Economic Committee, it was now our turn to reward the successful workshops.

The company's reward has three components. The first is a proclamation posted on the factory notice-board and on the door of the workshop itself, praising them for their diligence. The second is a cash bonus. This isn't actually paid until the end of the year, because it's calculated on the total output for the year as a whole. The Economic Committee simply gives a lump sum to each of the first finishers, but our bonus is meant to be divided up among the individual employees. Since the workshops have wildly differing numbers of employees the bonuses have to be calculated by a rather complicated formula. The reward that can be offered right away is a tea-party. Our union people lay in a supply of cakes, fruit and cigarettes, and all the members of the fêted workshop knock off for an afternoon of tea and chat in the meeting room as guests of the company.

These occasions are our own sort of harvest festival. Until I'd been to one it sounded so tame I couldn't believe anyone would actually show up. Now I'm convinced that these parties make a real impression. Unlimited food has a special appeal to adult Chinese who have all known real hunger. Not that they're hungry today or that they gorge themselves at the tea-party, but it has a symbolic impact. The employees rarely splash out on factory-made cigarettes, so the cigarettes distributed at the party make a refreshing change from the water-pipe. Then we take a lot of pictures and give copies out later. Employees don't normally own cameras. Most Chinese have few pictures of themselves, and those they do have are posed formal portraits. Candid shots talking and smiling with their workmates are a novelty their whole family will literally treasure.

When the foundry was under central planning, various snafus meant that these target-achieving celebrations were relatively rare. Recently, they've become more common. As Mr Go sips his tea and eats his peanuts he's enjoying respect from his lifelong co-workers that the managers in less stressful roles don't have the opportunity to savour.

5

Largesse

SALES and marketing are rather new concepts in China, and the terms are understood differently from their common meanings in a capitalist economy. Gold Land manufactures almost entirely for export, so I'm not as well qualified as others to explain the typical situation, but let me outline here what I've observed from the sales activities of our competitors and our suppliers.

This story, like so may others, must begin with central planning. It's a basic tenet of Communism that central planning is the fairest and most efficient mechanism for applying the nation's productive capacity to national development—for providing for each citizen according to his needs. In any economy one unit's output is another unit's input, right down to the final consumer, so planning and allocating leads the planner inexorably deeper and deeper into transactions at every level until he's controlling the distribution of all goods and services everywhere. In this situation sales and marketing are quite redundant, as no one in the system has any discretion as to what he consumes, in what quantity or from what source. Without this discretion the consumer is not susceptible to sales or marketing persuasion. The target of the marketing effort is not the consumer at all, but some bureaucrat deep in the state's planning machinery.

Of course, Communism has rarely been attempted in this pure form. Nevertheless, this is the model stressed in the Chinese education system and the avowed goal of the government and the party. It is this model which curses the efforts of Gold Land's Sales Manager to formulate a marketing plan.

This is not to suggest that selling is neglected in Chinese industry. In the Chinese system, as in most others, the prestige of the Factory Director is in rough proportion to the size of his factory, and factory size is measured first by turnover. So selling is a major management function. But the selling goes on in government offices, and it must proceed on two fronts simultaneously, for it would be senseless to generate additional 'orders' (output quota) without at the same time securing allocation of additional inputs—in our case, coke and pig iron. This is one reason why the marketing department of a Chinese business is usually known under a name along the lines of 'Purchasing and Sales Department'. In any business purchasing and sales must be closely co-ordinated, but under central planning they're really two sides of the same coin.

Another reason why purchasing and sales are grouped in a single department is that central planning invariably delivers the wrong mix of raw materials and output targets. So whatever the target, some material is always in short supply and another in temporary excess. One response is to hoard materials, but another essential response is to resell some of the items which are in surplus to acquire items which are short. This wouldn't be possible if the shortages had some sort of fundamental cause—in that case, all the factories would be short of the same key input. But in fact the usual cause is just planning mismatches or unplanned delays somewhere in the system. One foundry can be short of iron and overflowing with coke, while another foundry 100 km away but with different suppliers can be crying for coke while sitting on a big stock of iron. A meeting, a couple of banquets and a bit of trucking can promptly get both units moving. This happens, or threatens to happen, almost all the time, so the Purchasing and Sales Manager finds that both of his hats get plenty of wear.

There are many links in the chain from the iron mine in Guizhou Province to the consumer buying a cast iron wok in a Shanghai department store; but at the consumer's end of the

89

chain the mismatch situation is, in principle, no different. Central planning is meant to have arranged that each family receives a new wok every so many years. Mother has only to take her authorisation to one of the state stores and pick it up. The number of woks available in the local stores should equal the number of authorisations given in the local area, so only the last few consumers should have to make the rounds to discover which store has the last few of the stock.

Well, it's hard to believe that this system has ever worked anywhere, and it certainly doesn't work this way in China. In woks, as in almost everything else, the main market is a cash market. As recently as the early 1980s there were a lot of bare shelves, and wise shoppers bought ahead whenever items were available. By 1988, however, true abundance had spread to most of the heavily populated parts of the country. A particular type or brand of crackers might come and go in a particular city due to erratic distribution, but there are always crackers of some sort on sale. In this respect, China's experiments with a market economy seem to have pulled it ahead of some Eastern European countries. Things have not yet reached the point of extensive promotions, price reductions or even much consumer advertising, but that would be the logical next step if things are allowed to continue on their present course.

One area where real selling is necessary, however, is in the export market. Unfortunately, China's efforts here reflect the sales and marketing situation in the economy as a whole. Like most communist states, China has for many years sought to conduct foreign trade through state import and export agencies. These are organised industry by industry and are subdivided further into various provincial branches. So Guangdong Province has an import/export agency for light industrial products. The neighbouring province of Hunan has one as well. And each province also operates branches of parallel agencies for agricultural products, arts and crafts, textiles and quite a few other categories. If you're a foreign buyer looking for peanut oil you'll probably uncover at least half a dozen competing agricultural import/export agencies offering you the oil of various peanut-growing provinces.

And how do you uncover them? The country's lousy communications and transportation would make it pretty rough were it not for China's favourite marketing tool: the trade fair. There are lots of these all through the year, but the most famous are the Canton Trade Fairs held in autumn and spring. Twice a year, representatives from all the import/export agencies of all the provinces get together in Guangzhou to tackle the world's buyers and sellers of everything from nuclear reactors to macramé.

Foreign wheeler-dealers familiar with Houston's Offshore Technology Conference or Munich's ISPO sporting goods fair probably find the Canton Fair a bit of a joke. But Canton's most remarkable feature is that it's so deadly serious. There are no contests, no curvaceous beauties in skimpy costumes handing out samples. In fact, there are no samples. There's no need to tote around advertising-emblazoned plastic bags, as there is no litera-ture available about the products. There are no music videos, no flashing lights, no eye-catching signs. In fact, apart from a few consumer goods, China has no brand names.

Looking for sporting goods? The guidebook says Hall C, fourth floor, and sure enough, there they are. Barbells, basket-balls, bicycles—a whole floor full. As you enter, perhaps the first area is Henan Province. Displayed in no particular order is one sample of every article of sports equipment produced (or aspired to be produced) by any company in Henan. Seated around the tea tables are men (and a few women) in business attire who are prepared to discuss any item, negotiate with you, and take your order. Or if you're peddling carbon fibre fabrication technology they can talk about that too. A few steps further on and you pass into the area of Jiangsu Province. The display is about the same. In fact, the range of products, the designs, the quality, even the prices, are all just about the same. It's all very businesslike, but a Western trade fair is a lot more fun.

Buyers familiar with China will normally divide their orders among a number of these competing provincial agencies. Each agency will then divide the order further among the various producers in the province. This provides some assurance that at least some of the order will be delivered sometime. On the other hand, the foreign customer will never know exactly where the goods were made. So when quality problems arise, he can't expect much assistance. His only recourse is to claim against whichever import/export agency sent him that particular shipment; and then be prepared to prove it was from their shipment and not from another province. Not many foreign buyers pierce the veil and get out to see what's going on in the supplying factories, but the Hong Kong dealers make this their speciality and it has been the basis of their success.

As a foreign joint venture Gold Land has special rights to export its products directly without going through the state's import/export agencies. Our overseas marketing is handled in the conventional capitalist way by our Hong Kong partner and his overseas affiliates. It works well and gives us big market shares in our main product lines. But we nevertheless have a Sales Manager (he does no purchasing) charged with developing our rather minimal domestic business.

His name is Poon Wing Nin, and in many ways Mr Poon's personality fits the stereotype of the successful Western salesman. He's a cheerful, outgoing type—short and chubby, with the gift of the gab. He enjoys a bottle of beer and favours expensive, factory-made cigarettes. He's the skilful organiser of many of Gold Land's parties and banquets, and when the eating is over and the singing begins Mr Poon usually takes the floor as the master of ceremonies.

Mr Poon was appointed Sales Manager at the start of the joint venture, and at first he found his assignment baffling. His instinctive reaction was, 'They'll laugh at me. They'll laugh me right out of the office. They don't give orders to private foundries. They save them all for the state-owned work units.' Mr Poon's concept of selling was limited to visiting bureaucrats and negotiating plan allocations. 'Don't worry,' I said. 'We're not looking for government allocations. I want you to go out and get orders from private-sector firms.' Now I had him really worried. Mr Poon's image of a private-sector firm was an old lady selling oranges by the roadside.

With help from Hong Kong, Mr Poon eventually put together a pamphlet about the company and I showed him how he could generate a list of potential buyers for a mailing and follow-ups.

It's too early to say whether these efforts will bring us enough business to be worthwhile—Mr Poon's sales calls will be a new experience for the customers as well as for Gold Land. The effort has, however, got our staff thinking in terms of serving the customer. In most of Chinese business, this concept is conspicuously absent.

One of Mr Poon's first successes was our gas stove business. Gold Land manufactures small gas stoves for a local hustler who buys from us for cash and peddles them around the local area. Judging from his turnover he must be doing pretty well at it. But more usually these traders seem to deal in what should normally be considered stolen property. For example, one common market item around our area is plastic bags. One of the major supermarket chains in Hong Kong apparently has its plastic bags made in China, probably from raw plastic which it ships in from Hong Kong. The Chinese manufacturer seems to be able to squeeze extra bags out of the raw material provided, and somehow these end up on the Chinese domestic market where people use them in place of luggage when travelling and in place of boxes and cabinets for storage around the house. I would venture that the Chinese factory probably doesn't supply these pirate bags in any organised way. The employees simply steal any overruns for their private gain. All through the countryside it's easy to find tiles available in tile-producing areas, chinaware near porcelain factories and so on. Communism has taught the Chinese that private property is theft, and they seem to have taken their lessons to heart.

Despite our special status as an exporter Gold Land still has frequent opportunities to see the old system in action. Our sales are handled by our Hong Kong partners, but we buy all our raw materials in China. So we have an array of old-line Chinese state firms supplying us, and they do it in the old-line way. I can be sitting in the office drinking tea and trying to keep up with the mega-meeting when the cry goes up, 'Trucks in the courtyard. Guizhou licence plates.' A sales delegation has come to call.

Guizhou is one of China's poorest provinces, about three days by truck from our factory. It has little industry, but a lot of iron and coal is mined there, and the province provides much of our raw material. The business relationships have been carried over from the old days of the Gaozhou Foundry, but these state-run mines also remain interested in supplying the joint venture because our relatively steady receipts from Hong Kong mean that we can continue to pay our suppliers when state-owned units can't get cash. Of course, Gold Land too needs to maintain these relationships, so when they come to call we welcome them warmly as the old friends they are.

When we're all seated in the 'Meeting Guests Room' the visitors present us with some gifts from Guizhou—usually fruit or hot pepper sauce. Nothing unusual about that, but from that point on it begins to look less and less like a capitalist-style sales call. Mr Poon knows that it is considered *our* duty to entertain *them*. We are expected to accommodate them in our guesthouse, provide their meals, organise a banquet or two and help the driver prepare their truck for the trip home. When they leave we'll send them off with gifts of our Gaozhou speciality: bananas.

This custom makes no sense today. Why should the buyer be entertaining the seller? It's a carry-over from central planning, however, and there the reason is clear. A Factory Director operating under central planning must assure both his raw material allocations and his sales targets but, of the two relationships, raw materials take up much more of his time. The output targets are set at the beginning of the year and modified infrequently. Supplies, however, are a constant battle. Something is always late or the wrong quality, so the Factory Director is pleading with his suppliers all year long. In China this pleading takes the form of banquets, television sets and much more besides. To the men from Guizhou we are the goose that lays golden eggs, so they will resist any attempt to put our relationship on a more rational basis. The concept of the supplier serving the customer hasn't reached Guizhou yet. But that's no indictment. Even in pace-setting Guangdong Province the marketing philosophy remains confined to the marginal private sector.

If Gold Land were still a state foundry we too would have a few golden eggs rolling our way, laid by our one-time friends the import/export agencies. After taking an order for barbells from a Bulgarian gentleman at the Canton Trade Fair the import/export agency must now organise a production run at one of the province's foundries. In theory, this should be handled by central planning, but everyone has long since accepted that if they did it by the book the Bulgarians would soon be visiting India to buy their barbells. So the import/export guys get in their truck and begin visiting foundries likely to have the spare capacity, raw materials and skill to make the order. Much gift giving, banqueting and lying ensues, and after a week or two they straggle back to the office having divided the original order for 10 000 pieces into three sub-orders of 5000 pieces placed with different foundries.

You might expect that ordering 15 000 when only 10 000 are required could end in tears, and indeed you're probably correct, but not for the reason you have in mind. The real problem is that under scientific socialism, buyer and seller are unable to work together to ensure that China's barbells are preferred to India's. The import/export agency has learned through bitter experience not to trust the foundries.

While the agency's buyer is at the foundry, hospitality flows, solidarity is rampant, promises are sealed in blood. But as soon as his truck disappears over the hill another buyer for another product will take his place, or (worse yet) someone from the local government will call to expedite some brake drums for the state railways. If this happens the barbell order will soon be shunted to a siding.

On the other hand, the foundries know from bitter experience not to trust the agencies. They know that duplicate orders have been placed. They know that the agency always uses its own contract forms when ordering from the foundries and will never sign and return any contract or sales confirmation prepared by the foundry. As usual, the contract allows the agency to cancel all or part of the order at will and without compensation for any costs the foundry may have incurred. The foundry's selling price is also set by the agency, and then not until the conclusion of the contract. So most of the foreign exchange risk is passed back to the foundry. Worst of all, the import/export agency gets most of its orders at the few annual trade fairs, but these are not immediately passed on to the foundries. The agencies spoonfeed them

with a few weeks' work at a time, so the Factory Director has no
order backlog and can't do much production planning. He lives
from hand to mouth. This stop-and-go production is the worst
aspect of the whole system. The only mitigating factor is that
the agency will accept the first 10 000 barbells they receive. So
although a particular foundry's order may be for only 5000, if
production has gone smoothly the foundry can often just keep
on shipping and the agency will take the excess and reduce
someone else's order.

When we first started the joint venture I wasn't aware of these
practices. I was surprised that we didn't have a system for con-
firming orders in writing; but that was easily remedied. Then I
began hearing people making very odd statements. Mr Go began
arguing with the orders we were getting from the distributors.
He was asking for larger orders and for different items. I tried to
explain. 'What are they supposed to do? They're only passing on
the orders of the customers in Europe and America. Are you
going to criticise the Americans for what they choose to order?'
But Mr Go didn't seem to understand. On another occasion
some foremen proposed that we should continue to produce
certain items after the contract quantities had been finished.

Finally one day I understood their reasoning when we were
working on the problem of some goods which had been packed
in poor-quality cartons. Everyone agreed that the cartons were
not strong enough and that they would be crushed and broken by
the time they reached the wholesaler in Germany. Someone
suggested that rather than repack everything, we should simply
ship the weak cartons. If the wholesaler was dissatisfied, he could
repack the goods at his end in the cartons of his choice.

'Hey, come on,' I said. 'The customer isn't a factory. They
don't have dozens of employees sitting around waiting to repack
broken cartons.' 'I'll go help him!' someone cried. 'Very funny.
What's he going to use for cartons? Do you know how much
labour gets paid for filling cartons in Germany?' Several people
shouted, 'It's enough for me! I'll take it!' 'Listen,' I said. 'Even if
the wholesaler had the space and the materials, and even if he
had labour just sitting around waiting to repack our shipment,
why should he bother? Sure, if we bomb him with a surprise

shipment of rubbish we might force him to take some sort of drastic steps this year. But you can be 100 per cent sure this would be his last order.' 'Why so?' my managers innocently enquired. Unwilling to grace this with an answer, I delivered my ultimate Socratic salvo. 'Why should he pay us for rubbish when he can buy good stuff from India for the same price?' 'But,' they replied, 'he's *our* customer!'

Strange as it may seem, experienced managers were stumbling along on the unspoken assumption that all the world runs on some form of central planning. The marketing concept that the company exists to serve the needs of its customers was literally foreign to them.

Western marketers try to deliver to the customer a 'marketing mix'. But marketing is a pretty obscure concept in China, and with no concept of serving the customer the mix is to a large extent stripped down to a single, simple element: price. A first-time visitor to the Canton Trade Fair discovers this very quickly. Each delegation has a set of negotiating booths where they are prepared to negotiate and sign contracts. But just try discussing special colour schemes or packaging, unusual delivery arrangements or novel payment terms and see how far you get. The import/export agencies are not being stubborn. In the Chinese context any innovation, even sticking the label on the other end of the carton, is a major struggle. They would be foolish to let you believe otherwise. So in these negotiating booths negotiation means price negotiation and not much else.

When the agencies get out to the factories with the orders, again price is the main topic for discussion. Of course, the buyers need assurances about delivery dates, but both sides know that uncontrollable delays are normal. So lies are the common currency, and any attempt to really pin down delivery dates is probably a waste of time. The buyer invariably takes the line that all the other units have agreed to deliver this item at a certain price; take it or leave it. The factory talks about inflation and how the proposed price is out of line with items offered by some other import/export agency (the machinery agency, for example, instead of the light industrial products agency). The discussion is almost entirely formed in terms of how many cents per piece the price will be increased over last year's price. Negotiations can never end unsuccessfully, because enough of the central planning ethos remains to convince both sides that finally they have no choice but to work together to complete this order and every order, this year and every year. Each has his target, but delivering these products is their basic work assignment. There is no alternative.

No one in this entire pricing process, with the possible exception of the original foreign buyer, mentions a word about costs. To a large extent this is because no one really knows what they are. The 'social' costs of socialism are badly muddled up with variable costs at every level. Under a system of output targets and input allocation there is in any case not much that can really be considered a variable cost. And the prevailing standards of numeracy mean that no one operates very sophisticated allocation systems for their fixed costs. So price discussions are concluded pretty much without reference to costings.

This is not quite the recipe for disaster that it sounds. For each unit, profit is only one of its four targets. The key target is output, so the game plan (or, as the Chinese would say, the battle plan) is always to go for the turnover and worry about profits later. No unit is ever allowed to go broke; certainly not for turning out too many low-priced orders. At the national level this disregard of costs is just a resource-allocation problem. The state doesn't value its labour, its coal or even its scarce wood resources by reference to prices in the world's commodity markets. These things are deemed to cost what the state says they cost. At that level there still seems to be a certain reliance on the labour theory of value and other hoary Marxist dogma, so at the core of the onion you find no answer. When discussing prices, costs are simply not very helpful.

A capitalist sales manager should be able to apply his knowledge of shifts in the market to keep his company running in the right direction in its search for profits and growth. In China this is nonsense. A first-class sales effort can still help to increase turnover and profits, but the job is a pretty one-dimensional affair and offers the work unit as a whole no guidance about anything. Guidance is supposed to be the province of central planning; and since they do it badly or not at all, corporate strategy and national development begin to look like a random walk with very short steps. In China, as elsewhere in the communist world, people are beginning to notice. Even people who matter have been moved to reconsider, and this has led to China's recent experiments with joint ventures.

Announcements of new joint ventures usually discuss the modern technology that the foreign partner will bring to China, and there is sometimes acknowledgement that certain elements of modern Western management 'will be combined with the best Chinese practice' in the new company. But if you read the fine print of the joint-venture contract China has been willing to admit its need of a foreign joint-venture partner only because the partner promises to earn for China a lot of foreign exchange. It's not primarily the new technology that will allow these export sales, or even the new management practices; the really vital foreign contribution is an understanding of how to sell in the international market. Hong Kong is full of ambitious young entrepreneurs with years of international trading experience, including many with American MBAs. It's this marketing knowhow and sales experience, not modern management or technology, that is the key resource of successful joint ventures.

It's an open secret that China pirates foreign technology as a matter of national policy. The 'dime novel', for example, is not dead. A Chinese bookstore normally has one section closed to foreigners which sells reproductions of foreign works at prices which wouldn't even cover the cost of paper for a foreign publisher. During a ten-year joint-venture agreement the foreign partner is obligated to import a certain amount of foreign technology and to show the Chinese partner how to use it. If it works the Chinese tacitly intend to make their own domestic versions and spread them throughout the industry. Everyone understands this, but the foreign partners don't object. They know that, in the first place, obsolete technology is not China's major problem. And, with the best production capacity in the world, China will never pose a threat in international markets without a marketing and selling capability. That capability still seems a long way off.

Soon after our start-up, Gold Land imported and installed a

shot-blasting machine. Shot blasting is by no means high technology, and the particular unit we installed was by no means even at the forefront of modern practice. Nevertheless, it caused a stir in Gaozhou because the castings are fed through the machine on a conveyor, and this conveyor was the first and only conveyor in the entire foundry. Everyone noticed that with this machine three men could do the work of ten or twelve, and since shot blasting is noisy, dusty and generally unpleasant work everyone appreciated the improvement. In fact, this only eases our recruiting problem. But no matter, the big new machine generated a stream of tourists from the government and local factories and gave the local papers another anodyne topic to fill a few columns.

One of our government visitors looked the machine over, watched it run for a while and observed that much of the machinery was made of cast iron. 'These castings are not that complicated. You could make them, couldn't you?' 'Well, yes,' I replied. 'In fact, we're planning to make patterns of some of the key parts so we can cast our own spares. Importing from Taiwan is so complicated.' 'Yes, but I mean maybe we should consider copying the machine and selling it overseas to earn foreign exchange. After all, surely here we could produce it cheaper.' This remark pretty well typifies what I've seen of Chinese competitive strategy.

'I don't think we'd be very successful,' I ventured. 'The Taiwanese have invested in designing this machine. They probably protected their investment by registering the design. Maybe they even have patented certain features. Or the design might contain technology they licensed from somebody else for a fee.'

'Don't worry,' he replied. 'Those things don't apply in China. We can take care of it.'

'Yes, of course. But this is a labour-saving machine. Chinese foundries don't need it. You want to sell these machines overseas for foreign exchange. In capitalist countries, when the Taiwanese found we were selling copies of their designs they'd take us to court.'

'Hmmm.' He hadn't thought of that. 'Couldn't you change it a little bit?'

'Well, yes. But people who buy a machine like this want service,' I pointed out. 'We bought this one through a Hong Kong distributor . The Taiwanese manufacturer probably has a network of agents in all sorts of countries selling his machines. When it looks like they might make a sale they fly in engineers from Taiwan to figure out the customer's specific requirements. And then they send another bunch to install the thing. If it breaks down during the warranty period their guys come back and fix it.'

He got the point. With enough pull, a Chinese engineer might be allowed one trip abroad every two years, and then after six months or more of red tape.

China could make the machine. Of course it could. They could underprice the Taiwanese. Could they make a profit? Hard to say. The question is almost meaningless. But could they market the thing internationally? Not today. Not as long as, politically, China tries to remain a closed society.

So, as I said, sales and marketing are rather new concepts in the People's Republic, and the terms mean something a bit different from what we understand in a capitalist economy. As long as the Chinese cling to their special conception, the joint venturers are not worried that in teaching Chinese factories to make their products they'll be creating competitors.

101

6

Foraging

FORTY years of doctrinaire Marxism and Stalinism have left the Chinese business world encumbered with some unwieldy systems and practices which the reforms of recent years have not completely swept away. Perhaps the worst of these is the sclerotic procurement function that curses every Chinese enterprise. Strategies, organisations, personnel policies and most other aspects of business life have been restructured as part of the 'Four Modernisations', but procurement has been largely overlooked. Procurement continues to stagger along as a hybrid of central planning, so that it now constitutes a significant drag on the entire economy.

Under pure central planning the official duties of the Purchasing Manager (in fact, as we have seen, the Purchasing and Sales Manager) were simple indeed. A cast iron foundry with a certain output target would in theory be allocated sufficient supplies of coke, iron and other resources to fulfil its plan. Those quantities would appear in the output targets of certain smelters and coking plants and, on paper, the whole economy would work together smoothly to turn iron ore into cooking stoves. To the extent that the system ever worked smoothly, the foundry had no choice of suppliers, no control of the delivery schedule—almost no say in the entire process. The role of the Purchasing Manager, if he existed at all, was simply to co-ordinate the suppliers in executing the plan smoothly and on schedule.

Reality, of course, is quite different. In fact, the Purchasing and Sales Manager in a traditional work unit doesn't spend much time selling the products. Unless the factory manages vastly to exceed its targets all the output will be disposed of smoothly under the plan. Instead, it's virtually certain that at any given moment one or another of each factory's inputs will be out of balance with the others. The usual solution is inventory—keep big stocks of everything and hope that supplies will catch up before the stocks run out. But when that fails it's time for some purchasing and sales from the Purchasing and Sales Manager.

Or we may have the materials on hand, but their quality is too poor to use. The paint supplier delivers his paint, for example, but it's not quite the specified colour. The usual response to quality problems has always been to push on regardless, and if the customer complains simply blame the supplier. (That's why the paint company sent over a shipment they knew was the wrong colour rather than make the order again.) But export customers won't stand for it, and often quality problems are much more serious than off-spec paint. Quality variations which seem minor to the supplier sometimes simply cannot be processed into acceptable product. So here again it's the job of the Purchasing Manager to get out and find someone who has the right raw material.

It's unlikely, but there's always the off-chance that he might find a supplier who could be induced to trade some good materials for our off-specification lot. Or perhaps he can find a source who needs some products that our factory can make for him outside the plan. If so, he can quickly strike a barter deal. More likely, the supplier will need some special inducement to help us out. Corruption is thus an integral and inevitable part of a centrally planned economy. In fact, it's probably fair to say that under central planning an honest Purchasing Manager couldn't do his job.

Gold Land's Purchasing Manager is Ah Bo; and he got his job in an unusual way. For many years Ah Bo served the Gaozhou Foundry as a truck driver. He was a safe and skilful driver, but he was best known as a man who assiduously took care of his vehicle. 'His truck is his wife,' they used to say. His careful driving earned Ah Bo the task of driving for important visitors, and so he came to spend many travelling hours and many hotel nights with the managers of the foundry's Hong Kong customers.

One of those customers eventually became the joint-venture partner in Gold Land. Their managers had been trading in China for many years, and they were thoroughly familiar with the illegal payments demanded of any Chinese Purchasing Manager, but they were determined to resist these pressures as much as possible in the new joint venture. When it came time to set up Gold Land's new organisation, they had only one stipulation to impose. They wanted Ah Bo, a man they felt they could trust, as the new Purchasing Manager. He knew all the suppliers. He had visited them in their factories. But as a driver he had never been part of the system of under-the-table payments. So Ah Bo got a big promotion.

The joint venture had been running for about a month when Ah Bo, Mr Chow and I set off on a tour of introduction to some of our major suppliers. Our coke and iron suppliers are in rather underdeveloped parts of Guizhou and Guangxi provinces, and visiting them involves a rather long and uncomfortable tour by truck. As we set out, the truck was loaded up with bananas and some other Gaozhou local produce as gifts for our distant colleagues. But among the bananas I was surprised to find several colour TV sets.

Well, I wasn't surprised exactly. But I had rather hoped that as a joint venture Gold Land might have an excuse to turn over a new leaf and escape the cycle of bribing its suppliers. Bribery is supposed to be illegal, after all, and the directors of these large smelters are all important leaders in their provinces. 'Slowly,' I was assured. 'Slowly. You can't change the system overnight. Now that we're reorganised as a foreign joint venture, they'll treat us better, but only because we're bringing red fish instead of old comrades.' (The Hong Kong $100 note is red; the Chinese 100 yuan note bears a group portrait of four communist leaders from the Second World War.) We might expect better treatment from our suppliers than the old foundry had received, but only because our access to foreign currency and imported consumer goods would allow us to maintain our relationships so much better. Seen in that light, my hopes looked pretty unrealistic.

I saw just how unrealistic a few months later when I was involved in discussions with a supplier of a different kind: the Electricity Supply Bureau. As most parts of China are short of generating capacity, ordinary factories must maintain a continual lobbying effort to minimise their share of the power cuts. In the past the foundry's relationship with the Electricity Bureau had always been based on family ties—one of our managers had a relative working there. But with the joint venture the relationship was moving on to a new basis, and that's why I was involved. It all stemmed from our desire to upgrade our electrical system. The previous 460 kW supply was completely inadequate, and we proposed to upgrade to 2000 kW immediately, with provision to install another 2000 kW line later. This would make us the largest electricity consumer in the area.

As in any country, installing new capacity like that must be co-ordinated with the electricity supply authorities. As in most countries, their inspectors check all new equipment and permit its connection to the public distribution grid. But in China we needed their deeper involvement in the process, because without them it would be difficult for us to buy the equipment for our new installations.

Upgrading our electrical system involved rewiring the factory and installing new circuit breakers and load-control equipment. But the biggest renewal involved replacing the main transformer which steps the high voltage of the public mains down to the voltage that our machines use in the factory. It was this old transformer, with its maximum capacity of 460 kW, which limited the whole plant's electricity consumption. The new 2000 kW transformer is by no means a giant transformer. Even in China many transformer factories make them, but most of them are sold to electricity bureaux to provide the power for a town or a part of a city. There was no reason in principle why Gold Land couldn't approach a transformer factory and buy one directly; it was just that we had no 'relationship' with such a factory. China is trying to expand its power supply. Lots of new equipment is being installed, and the transformer factories consider themselves busy. We might approach a transformer factory

105

directly and eventually get our transformer, but it would go a lot more smoothly if we were introduced by our local Electricity Supply Bureau.

The Gaozhou electricity bureaucracy was also anxious to help us install our new capacity, but I quickly realised that their motive wasn't just bureaucratic empire-building. Our discussions started with a series of banquets. Then there were potential business trips, probably to be made using our air-conditioned truck instead of public transportation. But the real attraction revealed itself in the course of the negotiations. They proposed to collude with us in swindling their own work unit, the Electricity Supply Bureau. A factory pays for its power on the basis of its metered consumption, but in addition there is a flat monthly charge based on the factory's installed capacity. They proposed to under-report our new capacity and split with us our savings on the monthly charge.

This was a pretty crude swindle. I suppose the rank and file of the Electricity Bureau don't have too many opportunities to ride the gravy train, so they didn't have any more sophisticated proposals ready to offer. It's lucky for them that we didn't accept their suggestion, as a year later the Tiananmen Square massacre precipitated an anti-corruption drive in which their unsophisticated conspiracy could easily have been used to set them up as scapegoats when the time came for Gaozhou to deliver its quota of miscreants. Instead, our Board of Directors took this problem off my hands and declined their offer in a rather clever way. They offered them a much bigger deal. They offered to help them import some used generating equipment from Germany. This offered them a whole new range of legitimate trips and banquets, including a treasured trip to Hong Kong.

I probably found out about this particular swindle only because the perpetrators were such inexperienced swindlers. Wilier heads would have set up their scheme in such a way that it would never have come to my attention. I trust my Gold Land managers. I have to, because I know they have ample opportunities to divert company funds to their own pockets through swindles like this one. The managers all clearly understand that it won't be tolerated, and one who was discovered in a similar scam has already found himself back on the casting floor. But if there are others who continue to abuse this trust they have so far been able to conceal their activities. In the prevailing Chinese business culture it seems many would be prepared to assist a crook by looking the other way. I have this Electricity Bureau example to present only because the conspirators were particularly naive.

In recent years the iron grip of the plan has loosened considerably, but much of its legacy remains. In our first two years we have reviewed and modernised the work of every department. Even the union has made some major changes. But our Purchasing Department, even though it's no longer Purchasing and Sales, has probably changed least of all. Whatever changes we might like to make, purchasing operates outside Gold Land in the general economy. If we are to continue to procure effectively we can't let our purchasing practices get too far out of step with the prevailing business culture, however corrupt it may be.

Perhaps the single most distinguishing feature of Chinese business culture is the 'relationship'. Marxism has outlawed business relationships based on competitive advantage, but they have failed fully to replace this basis with central planning. So the Chinese have evolved a business culture modelled on the strong Chinese extended family. In a Chinese family there is a strict hierarchy led by the father and eldest son. Relatives all have detailed titles along the line of 'my father's younger brother' which convey a distinct hierarchy of all the siblings, cousins, aunts and uncles relative to the speaker. In business you very often hear these titles, particularly older brother and younger brother, applied to business colleagues in an attempt to explain a relationship. In communist theory everyone is working together under central planning for the common good. But when central planning breaks down the common good is a pretty indistinct criterion for deciding whether the one available railway wagon should be despatched to unit A or unit B. In this situation relationships take over in guiding the decision, and they put a certain order, however inefficient, into the allocation of resources.

Our foundry employs about seven or eight full-time buyers. I don't know the exact number because most of them return to the foundry only once or twice each year. The rest of their time is spent on the premises of our suppliers. When there is something to be purchased they handle the formalities, but their primary job is relationship-building. They live in our suppliers' guesthouses, give them gifts, invite them to dinners and generally try to build the atmosphere of mutual obligation which is the essence of the Chinese business relationship. Each major relationship is maintained by an individual buyer, and the Factory Director is treated as if he were our only supplier. We help him increase his allocation of railway wagons, we help him fudge his shipment figures to meet his plan targets, and we still slip him cash or consumer goods under the table from time to time. On one occasion when we were short of iron our buyer was able to call on an individual smelter manager at his house with 5000 yuan in cash and immediately managed to free up a few weeks' supply. That's about US$1000, or two years' salary and bonuses for a Factory Director.

It's all necessary because there is no orderly market where buyers can openly compete for scarce resources. Every visitor to China has seen the same process in miniature at the railway stations. Rail travel is so cheap that it's vastly overused. The excess demand is regulated by long, unruly queues at the ticket windows. But business travellers, party and government officials, and foreign tourists don't stand in these lines. They buy their tickets through official contacts (like the China Travel Service) and other unofficial ones. They pay more, and they provide various cigarettes and other gifts to get the seats they want. With no capitalist market to regulate distribution, relationships take over.

One Western convention which I've tried to introduce at Gold Land is the purchase order. I've tried to sketch for Ah Bo how convenient it would be if we could sign an annual contract with each of our suppliers and then simply send him a purchase order each time we would like him to send us a shipment under the contract. He listens to me politely, and I think he understands how convenient it is in capitalist economies. But he's entirely unconvinced that the foundry will ever be able to do it that way. His scepticism is probably well founded. Mailing off purchase orders is no way to maintain the relationships with our suppliers.

And as long as coke and iron are in short supply only the relationship motivates our suppliers to take care of us, their little brother, rather than some other unit. So whatever our joint-venture status our purchasing continues to play by the special rules of the Chinese marketplace.

A joint venture, in theory, operates entirely outside the residual central planning system. In fact, central planning continues to influence in peripheral ways even a private company like Gold Land. One direct impact is through rail services. Iron and coke must be shipped by rail, and the allocation of railway wagons remains largely under central planning. China has no basic shortage of either iron or coke, but the foundry often encounters shortages because no rail cars are available to bring supplies to the factory. The smelters and coking plants are normally state-owned enterprises subject at least in part to central planning. As such, they are allocated a certain supply of rail cars to ship the planned portion of their output, but the free market portion is left to fend for itself in the free portion of the market for rail cars.

The origin and status of this free market in rail cars is obscure, and it's in the interest of many people that it should remain so. Until I can quiz someone from the railway ministry I have to speculate that it works as follows. China controls railway freight charges at artificially low levels, so work units overuse the service and the country is chronically short of rail cars. Despite the shortage, the nation lacks the technology to keep track of each of its cars individually. A particular regional rail centre probably has monthly targets to deliver a certain number of rail cars to each of a list of state enterprises in the region. It has trains out to neighbouring regions each day, and it has trains coming in. Beyond that it has an approximate count of the cars in the region and where they are to be found. With this information it tries to meet its targets.

The shipper has a plan allocation of rail cars each month to meet his output targets, but actual availability often differs from the plan. He must stay in constant contact with the district rail yard to ensure that he receives a share of whatever cars are available. Up to a point he can do this by invoking his plan allocation, but this argument alone will never be enough. In conditions of general shortage, one month with less cars than planned must be compensated by an over-plan quantity in the next month. And even then, this will ship only the in-plan portion of the factory's output. What about all the private-economy sales?

There are three basic solutions. One is hoarding. Grab every available car and keep it on your siding until it's needed. A second is overloading. Overloading the planned cars will leave a few left over for private-economy shipments or for catching up on last month's shortfall. But the third possibility is to call on the gentleman at the railyard who, in the last analysis, decides how many empty cars will be shunted on to your siding tomorrow morning. This man has whatever information is available about the supply of cars entering the district, which factories are not using their full allocation, what stock of cars is loading or unloading in the district, and what might become available when. He's a busy man, with a complex job and some control of a scarce, and therefore valuable, resource. He has the potential to be very rich. If you really need rail cars, you can often obtain some by making him richer.

Gaozhou is not on the rail line, so we ship our products by truck. Nevertheless, I must admit that Ah Bo and his buyers are also players in the great rail car game. For we must bring our coke and iron supplies by rail to Maoming, a city about 50 km away, and truck them in from there.

As a private-sector joint venture we must purchase and ship our raw materials entirely outside the plan. It should by now be clear that if the Purchasing Manager simply called the supplier and placed an order, or sent him a purchase order form, Gold Land would never receive anything. The coke and iron are in plentiful supply, but to get the rail cars it's necessary to be on the spot, wheeling and dealing. So in fact we maintain a list of four or five suppliers for each of these key raw materials, and one of our buyers is permanently stationed at each of those eight or ten smelters.

Our buyer's first step is to pay cash in advance for the iron or coke. This gives us a place in the queue of buyers hanging about the supplier's guesthouse, each waiting for a prepaid shipment not yet delivered. Every few days the supplier receives another batch of rail cars. Some he will use to fulfil his targets under the plan. Any surplus is up for grabs among the prowling buyers. The result is a sort of auction. There's no organised ceremony with an auctioneer, but the buyers compete to offer the most tempting inducements to receive some of the available cars.

Alternatively, the enterprising buyer might try approaching the railway officials directly. This is hard work, as they will normally prefer to deal with their local factories. But money talks in this situation, and in any case the buyer normally stays in one factory for months or years, so he becomes a long-term customer.

The outcome of these auctions is inherently unpredictable. The supply of cars is highly variable for a start, but as in all auctions the clearing price depends on how badly all the competing buyers need the cars. Gold Land's only defence is to keep generous stocks in our factory and buyers at several smelters widely scattered around China. Despite this, the delivered price of our raw materials can vary as much as 15 per cent from month to month.

In terms of value most of our purchasing centres on these main raw materials. But China's feeble distribution system makes it difficult to allocate most of our purchasing effort to the big-value items. Take, for example, sanitary napkins. If you want only a few, it's normally possible to buy them in the shops of Gaozhou. At the other extreme, if you need a few hundred thousand you can get those too—by the laborious expedient of sending someone to the paper factory to negotiate an out-of-plan sales contract. But in between these extremes a wholesale distribution system is almost entirely lacking. The distributor who buys by the tonne and sells in cartons of a few dozen doesn't exist. Sanitary napkins are a recent innovation in China, and when they first caught on a few years ago they were so popular that they quickly became a standard fringe benefit provided by factories to their workers. Even a minor factory must provide thousands of them each month—just the sort of quantity that's too big to find in the retail market and too small to buy from the manufacturer.

111

To solve this problem, and also as a weapon in the birth-control programme, distribution of sanitary napkins became the responsibility of the union. Each company's union is affiliated with the local union organisation of the city and county. These bodies pool the napkin requirements of all the local factories into truckload quantities, and they then receive an in-plan allocation from the manufacturer. These days, the retail market seems to be supplied mainly by leftovers from the in-plan workers' monthly rations which they have sold to private traders for cash.

At first I didn't realise that the procurement situation was so unusual, and it seemed that two or three times a week I was stumbling over some seemingly trivial procurement problem. The employees mentioned, for example, that the gloves we were issuing weren't tough enough for handling sharp, rusty scrap iron. So I asked our Safety Officer to try a different style. He agreed with me, but for some mysterious reason nothing happened. Weeks later, the employees were still using the same gloves and having the same problems. Finally I got around to really following up and learned what had been going on.

There was no official channel for buying hundreds of pairs of gloves every month in the Gaozhou market. On the other hand, it just so happens that there are several glove factories in Gaozhou filling export contracts for Hong Kong distributors. The most effective way to change our style of gloves was to arrange for some of these local factories to sell us their rejects and overruns, and in fact to arrange some 'special overruns' to divert some of the Hong Kong customers' raw materials into gloves to be sold to us for cash. The only problem was that we had to wait until the next production run to implement the plan. Until we came along there had been no way to dispose of these export-quality gloves around Gaozhou, so all the rejects and overruns were shipped off with the orders. Next run, they began setting them aside for us.

Well, that wasn't exactly the solution I'd anticipated, but we did eventually change gloves. I suppose the Hong Kong customer was being cheated no more than before and was at least getting more consistent quality. But at Gold Land it alerted me to the problems of wholesale distribution in China and suggested an idea for stabilising and diversifying our cast iron business. Why not, I reasoned, set our company up as a wholesale distributor of iron and coke?

There are dozens of small cast iron foundries around Gaozhou and the surrounding counties. All live from hand to mouth, buying truckload quantities of pig iron and coke from larger foundries and wherever they can find them. They are not large enough customers and don't have enough buying personnel to maintain good relationships with several smelters, so most must speed up and slow down in response to the availability of raw materials from just one or two sources. As quality from these sources varies, they have no other stocks to blend in; so the quality variations affect their operations and the quality of their output. If a wholesaler were to keep physical inventories of coke and pig iron ready for cash sales in truckload quantities he could charge a premium price, but these small operators would often feel compelled to buy. And if Gold Land operated the distributorship it would not only give us some control of our smaller competitors but, by augmenting the volume of our own purchases, the new business would also give us more influence with the smelters and the railways. No one else would be able to copy this initiative because we would finance the stocks with investment from our Hong Kong partners. No local competitor could raise the finance domestically. It seemed a fine way to get some extra mileage from our existing purchasing network.

My idea was well received. The Hong Kong board members saw my reasoning at once and began preparing the ground with some of the various government agencies that would have to provide the land for our stock yard and in various other ways bless our efforts. My managers and the Chinese board members were a little surprised at first. They had never heard of such an idea. State-owned factories have no concept of a business strategy and they rarely diversify in this way. The whole concept of a distribution business required some getting used to, although they could see the practical advantages of creating such a service.

The idea gathered momentum for a while and then gradually died. I suspect that it was strangled, not by any practical problem, but principally by unease in the local Communist Party. I never met any party official in Gaozhou who publicly condemned the new private sector on ideological grounds. Indeed, opening up to private business is officially endorsed as one aspect of the 'Four Modernisations'. But private wholesale distribution of such basic state resources as coke and pig iron would be a fundamental challenge to communist orthodoxy. It was simply too liberal an experiment for the small-town party apparatus to sanction independently. If the wind should ever shift they could be blown away by charges of bourgeois liberalism and sabotaging socialism. The proposal was simply too innovative for them to sanction.

Of course, in any country, East or West, the Purchasing Manager finds himself devoting a lot of time to sourcing special one-off purchases. When the radio factory suddenly needs to buy a pump the Purchasing Manager can find this pretty challenging. But in a capitalist economy he at least knows where to turn for help. As a first step he has the yellow pages, and probably he keeps a library of 'buyer's guides' listing all the suppliers of various types of equipment. Once he has found the telephone numbers of a few sources he can count on their salesmen to give him a basic education in pump buying without the need to leave his office. Sadly, in China, none of this exists.

The most critical lack is advertising. In the ideal centrally planned economy, advertising really would be unnecessary and wasteful. But in reality every firm must operate at least partly outside the plan, and unfortunately advertising has not grown to meet this need. So if you're not normally a pump user, the first step in buying a pump is to begin asking friends, neighbours and fellow employees if they know anyone who works in a unit such as a chemical factory which uses a lot of pumps. Armed with one or two introductions the next step is to drop around for a chat, distribute a few cigarettes and try to learn something about the pump industry. These visits continue until you've accumulated the names of three or four pump factories that probably make something suitable. Then it's on to the train and away you go to call on the pump factories. There, at last, you should probably be able to meet someone who can understand the original pumping problem and recommend a solution. Dinners are bought, drinks drunk and a deal struck. It's all quite a struggle.

Unfortunately, the difficulty is not entirely limited to unusual, one-off purchases. A foundry buys a lot of paint. Cast iron rusts easily, especially in the humid climate of south China, so virtually every piece we cast has to be painted before shipping. On the other hand, many of the castings we make are only parts for various products which will be painted again after assembly, or items like agricultural machinery where the appearance of the paint job is not of much importance. So Gaozhou Foundry had always bought its paint, tonnes of it each month, from a small local paint factory. It was the cheapest finish available, and always black. Each piece we made was dipped in this stuff and thrown in a pile on the floor to drip dry—painting at its cheapest and nastiest.

But once we started diversifying our product line one of the first new ideas was a line of garden furniture. Not only was it specified in white and green as well as black, but the appearance of the finish was of great importance and, worst of all, it required baked enamel paint. The paint the foundry had been buying was inadequate, and our little local supplier couldn't supply anything suitable. Thus began our three- or four-month search for a new paint supplier.

No one really wanted to supply us with the paint we needed— at least not at the outset. We had not yet started to make this garden furniture. We could not expect to buy an enormous quantity of this baked enamel paint in the first year. We could not significantly help any paint factory to make its targets. If there had been a suitable factory around Gaozhou county, we could have asked our friends in the government to help ensure that we were allocated a bit of production capacity. But unfortunately the only paint factory in Gaozhou was the one depending on our orders for the cheap black stuff. So we couldn't even take that business away from them to increase our bargaining power with another factory. That would only have aggravated our government friends. So we had to set out on our own to find a supplier.

The first step was to ask around among the other factories in Gaozhou to see if anyone could introduce us to a baked enamel supplier. No luck there. Our contacts were fertiliser plants, a sugar refiner, a rubber factory, glove makers, electronics fabricators—dozens of factories, but no one buying baked enamel paint. So we went further afield and asked our Hong Kong partners to speak to other business contacts in China for some names. We visited the Canton Trade Fair and asked around. Once, when invited to visit a factory in a distant county, I went around writing down the addresses on the pails of paint in their warehouse. By these various techniques we eventually assembled the names of four or five factories making enamel paint around Guangdong Province.

In any other country that would be the end of the story. This is not a one-off purchase. Gold Land is going to buy this new paint in tonnage quantities for years to come. The paint factories should be happy to hear from us, and our problem should be solved. Unfortunately it doesn't work that way in China.

All of these factories are making paint under central planning, and most are probably also selling part of their output in the cash market to various companies like Gold Land. In a general way they would like to expand their business, but on a day-to-day basis they're probably behind in their deliveries for all the usual reasons and, though the factory may be operating at 60 per cent of its rated capacity, each feels that it's going flat out in terms of its realistic production potential. No one has a sales force out scavenging for new business. A postal request for a catalogue might prompt them to send a card of colour chips, but they would be just as likely to read the letter bemusedly and file it in the wastebasket.

If we were to get any further in our quest Gold Land now had to convince some of these suppliers that we were worth talking to. In fact, we weren't worth talking to. Not for that initial order, anyway. We should have been talking to a wholesale paint distributor, if such a thing existed. For this first order we could make ourselves interesting to a paint factory only by the usual tactic of gifts and banquets, and by suggesting that we had access to the red fish—hard foreign currency. This usually gets them to prick up their ears, but it has to be done in person. So we had to send one of our buyers on tour.

Our buyers, of course, knew nothing about paint. For years they had bought the same paint from the same company month after month. Even in their private lives they had probably never had occasion to buy and use a can of paint. If they had ever repainted their living quarters they undoubtedly did it with whitewash—the standard architectural finish in this part of China. In a capitalist economy this ignorance wouldn't have been a serious problem. They need only have explained that we wanted to make cast iron tables and chairs for outdoor use, and the paint company's salesmen would gladly have educated them about the advantages of various paint formulations for this application. But a Chinese paint company doesn't really have salesmen; just as Gold Land has only a Sales Manager but no salesmen. So our buyers had to deal with the senior management of these paint companies, and they would be better able to get their attention if they could state their business clearly. So before setting off on our quest we first requested some paint formulations and performance specifications from our overseas customers. They're garden furniture distributors, not manufacturers, but nevertheless it was easier for them to get this information than it was for us.

We eventually struck up a relationship with a paint company that could provide what we needed. This particular contact started at the Canton Trade Fair where one of the import/export agencies was trying to sell paint for export and was distributing sheets of colour chips with the name and address of the factory mentioned on the bottom. (This divulging of their source was a slip-up by the import/export agency.) Fortunately for us the factory had recently expanded its capacity, so they were seeking new business. And the samples they provided seemed to work acceptably. Eventually we arranged to buy a tonne of their paint for a test run in the new oven we had built to bake the finish.

This test run was crucial to our decision to buy their paint in production quantities. They were aware that we knew nothing about paint and had just built this oven. Normally you would expect the paint company to be anxious to participate in the test, to ensure that we didn't misjudge their paint through our own ignorance about applying it and baking it properly. With this in mind we invited them to send someone to observe the test.

They replied that they would be delighted to help. In fact,

their General Manager and Sales Manager would both attend, assisted by a technician. Could we please send a truck (900 km) to pick them up, and prepare food and accommodation for them? This sounded a bit rich to me, so I cabled to suggest that we didn't really need such massive assistance, and couldn't they just send their technician on the bus? We would pay his expenses. After a couple of exchanges of telegrams the answer became clear: three or none. You want help; you give us a trip. Take it or leave it.

We took it. And with their advice the test was a success. But I asked Ah Bo to keep looking for another supplier. 'If he's going to treat us that way, we'll buy his paint for the time being. But let's see if we can't find somebody else with a more co-operative attitude.' Ah Bo couldn't understand my dissatisfaction. It seemed normal to him that we had asked the paint company for a favour, and we had no reason to feel offended by their reply. Further, having entertained them and worked together on the test run, we had now built up the all-important 'relationship'. With this in place we were in a position to work smoothly with this supplier for years to come. How could I be dissatisfied?

I didn't appreciate his line of reasoning at the time, but in retrospect I can see that he was right. The Japanese also emphasise long-standing relationships and the generation of mutual obligations in their business culture, but in China the lack of much of a profit motive makes the relationship the key to any sort of business transaction. It's not a system that Western business feels very comfortable with, but the rules of baseball won't get you far on the cricket pitch.

In a similar episode I tried my hand at what macroeconomists might call technology transfer. Right from the start, I had been aggrieved by all the manual material-handling that was going on in the foundry. Cast iron parts are heavy, and as they moved through the various manufacturing operations they were repeatedly being picked up from a pile on the floor, processed and then thrown back on to another pile. One of my approaches to improving the situation was to introduce conveyors.

From the purchasing point of view this was a problem worse than anything which had gone before. The foundry didn't have any conveyors, so we didn't have a relationship with any conveyor-manufacturing unit and the whole thing had to be researched from scratch. From my point of view we were starting even below scratch, because at least everyone had been familiar with the concept of paint, or transformers or gloves. The new paint was different from the old, but at least everyone could discuss it in terms of how it differed from the stuff we had been using for years. The conveyor was a whole new concept.

Most conveyors are driven by an electric motor, which limits their utility in Gaozhou. To introduce the concept in its simplest, most flexible and most useful form I decided to start with a few lengths of roller conveyor. This is the gadget used to unload beverage trucks in most developed countries. It's just a row of rollers or little ball-bearings on a frame about 3 metres long. Set it up with a slope, put something at the top and it zips down the rollers pulled by gravity. With no motor and no rubber conveyor belt these conveyors are quick and easy to set up and require almost no maintenance.

The first step in the purchasing process was to find someone in China who was using a conveyor of this type so that we could ask him the name of the supplier. But unless I was intending to do all the looking myself there was a before-the-first step, which was to explain to some of the other Gold Land people what I had in mind—what they were supposed to be looking for. After various attempts at sketching and building little models out of chopsticks I eventually realised that a roller conveyor is built just like an abacus. That made it easy. After sliding a few books and boxes of tea down some abacuses everyone had the picture. Then we fanned out to work units around the Gaozhou area on the trail of technology transfer.

The search eventually took about six months. We tried all the factories we knew, then moved on to various likely possibilities such as soft-drink bottlers. We eventually met people who had seen them on trips to Hong Kong, but we never found one in China.

What eventually got things moving was a report from our Guangzhou shipping office, where someone reported that the truck bringing empty containers in from Hong Kong had a length of roller conveyor strapped behind the cab. We sent a man with a tape measure, and during the truck's next visit we noted all the details of this high-tech secret weapon. We then had quite a hunt for the right kind of ball-bearing, but eventually we were able to ask one of our machine shop subcontractors to fabricate a test section for us. That first sample didn't actually work too well, as we hadn't used strong enough materials in the copy. But once the foremen and employees saw the principle in action they quickly realised how useful it could be. We made some improved models, and now other work units are copying from us.

The sad part about all of this is that somewhere in China there is probably a factory making quite serviceable roller conveyors. Some Sinologist reading this will probably write to tell me that the Chinese invented the roller conveyor in 1024 BC. But without any proper advertising or any distribution channels it took six months of hunting before we could begin reinventing the wheel.

The common element in all of this is market inefficiency. Factories are not getting the supplies they need, goods are being sold at inappropriate prices, and innovation and modernisation are stifled by the difficulty of doing anything new. Most of all, these inefficient and badly informed markets are controlled by an empire of individuals with personal power to allocate scarce resources. Their cigarettes, cognac and motorcycles are a private tax on transactions at every level. It's all illegal; everyone agrees it must stop. But right now no one can imagine how. In the absence of a really free market these fixers are in fact performing a service in allocating scarce resources. And they are being rewarded for it. It's only with their help that the system staggers along.

7

In search of the bottom line

A CHINESE factory makes an extensive monthly report to its supervising Economic Committee. This shouldn't be surprising, as central planning would certainly need all sorts of up-to-date statistics if it were ever to function as intended. In fact, though, the reports aren't of much help to the planners. The problem is not in their volume, but in the quality of the information they contain.

Gaozhou Foundry was typical of almost all the small and medium-sized factories of rural China in having no trained bookkeepers or accountants on its staff. Mr Ho Hak, the foundry's Accounting Manager, is still Gold Land's Accounting Manager today. He was promoted from the casting floor after he completed a television course in bookkeeping. With that training he could cope with the Gaozhou Foundry's monthly report and get it out on time, but his television course didn't really train Mr Ho in accounting fundamentals. Now the joint venture calls for some new bookkeeping techniques, and Mr Ho is having trouble keeping up. He makes no bones about it. He admits, with his nervous smile, that all he can do is work hard and try to learn as he goes along from the trained accountants of our Hong Kong partner. You have to sympathise with him.

His staff are diligent young ladies, graduates of the local secondary school. (This puts them among our best-educated staff.) They are literate and quick with an abacus. But they've learned

121

most of what they know from Mr Ho, or from television courses. In the days of the Gaozhou Foundry this crew prepared a monthly report of 25 or 30 pages for the local Economic Committee. These reports were heavy with data but very short on analysis. The only consistent analytical approach was to compare each number with last year, or with this year's planned result.

A capitalist financial report normally begins with either the balance sheet or the income statement. Central planning offers no options on this or on any other question of the report's format. Every report from every unit begins with this month's tax return.

Income tax in China is charged not on profits, and not on value added, but as a percentage of sales. So the first and most important calculation begins with the shipments of the month, corrected by various minor adjustments and used to calculate the firm's tax liability. This is followed by reports about equipment purchases and maintenance spending, employment figures, and finally, on page seven, the income statement.

Profit has a sensitive position in Marxist theory. But, despite the labour theory of value, a Chinese factory's monthly profit calculation is not grossly at variance with what a capitalist accountant might calculate. The fixed assets are depreciated on a straight line from their historical costs. At first glance the main difference seems to be a lack of accruals and amortisations. Taken as a package the report is a lot like a Chinese machine—overdesigned but at the same time oversimplified. There is really little choice about this. Even percentages are not easy to calculate on an abacus, and operating accruals and suspense accounts would be beyond the abilities of the people which most factories are able to recruit as their bookkeepers. An experienced capitalist manager would find the monthly report a good starting point in running the factory, but the average Chinese probably doesn't pay much attention to it.

In the first place, the typical manager has never been trained to understand accounting terminology. At the same time, he understands that his supervisors at the Economic Committee don't pay much attention to the report either. They can't study 30 pages each month from every unit in the county. The manager knows that he's measured on four simple results: turnover, investment, employment and profit. The tax implications are another reason why, as we have already seen, turnover is by far the most important of these. The monthly report was designed by the central planners, and they're free to study it if they wish. But neither the manager nor the Economic Committee finds it very helpful in meeting the four key targets. As a result, the monthly report becomes a 30-page monthly tax return. It must be done on time, and it must be right; but it's not an important tool in the management process. The work of the Accounting Department is accordingly lightly regarded. The results are about what you would expect.

Pricing, judging from the example of the Gaozhou Foundry, is done with no clear idea about costs. There is no management accounting system, so no one has any concept of how the very substantial fixed costs of the iron rice bowl should be allocated to the various products. The actual practice has been to regard all costs as fixed costs. After all, the factory has a planned output target. One way or another, the employees must turn out so many tonnes of product per month. With the existing equipment, each tonne of product will require a certain amount of pig iron and a certain amount of coke. Purchased parts from the subcontractors must be calculated carefully, but everything else can be considered fixed cost and priced at so much per tonne.

Of course it's wrong, but in a communist economy the error doesn't matter much. Profit is really the least of the four targets. In any case, the foundry can't refuse work, even if it's unprofitable. If the profits turn out negative it's considered fair enough to point to the 'customers' and say that they have set the prices too low. In theory, the foundry, its suppliers and its customers are all one big happy socialist family eating from the same national pot. One unit's loss is another's gain, but it's all in the family.

With units operating this way the pricing system is emasculated. Prices convey little information about value, so it becomes impossible to tell efficiency from waste. The authorities can report a 10 per cent increase in tractor output, but only guesses about whether they should have been producing motorcycles instead. Next year, when both the tractor factory and the motorcycle factory ask for new investment, there will be no basis for allocating the new resources except someone's connections and influence.

Cost control is another area where a capitalist manager would expect to get a lot of help from his Accounting Department. But it doesn't work that way in most Chinese enterprises. The problem is twofold. Basically the Chinese Factory Director is the Emperor figure in his work unit, and most directors are very reluctant to delegate. Whatever cost data they receive from their bookkeepers, such Factory Directors are still limited by their physical capacity to get around and fix individual inefficiencies. So if they could get perfect cost analysis it would just be a thorn in their flesh—a constant reminder of their inability to run the entire factory personally. But in real life the Accounting Department is unable to provide the necessary data anyway.

Trained Chinese accountants understand about budgets and variance reports. They have studied costing systems and can probably explain the theory behind various systems of overhead cost allocation. But these trained accountants are in short supply. As university graduates they can work in Guangzhou or Shanghai. The smaller work units don't have these trained personnel. They don't have computers to churn out timely variance reports; they don't have bookkeepers who know enough theory to prepare the reports by hand; they don't have paper to write them on; and they don't have managers who know how to read them.

Investment decisions, in contrast, are much too important to allow much input from the Accounting Department. Investment is one of the four key targets, and success in this area consists of increasing the unit's stock of machinery, not improving return on investment. Under central planning almost any major equipment acquisition will require approval and assistance from the local government's Economic Committee, so the key to scoring well on the investment criterion lies in cultivating the favour of the local planners. There is no role for the bookkeepers in that process, so the Accounting Department finds itself excluded from financial management.

The most serious effect of this exclusion is that many Chinese factories have little concept of the costs involved in carrying stocks. The managers tend to recognise costs only on a cash basis, so they recognise that they are paying a lot of interest charges but don't consider liquidating stocks as a solution.

When the Gaozhou Foundry was absorbed into Gold Land we conducted a complete inventory and found tonnes and tonnes of very old castings stored here and there around the factory. All could be 100 per cent recycled in place of buying new pig iron, but Mr Chow had never considered this because the foundry carried these items on the books at their original sales value. In using them for scrap they would have been obliged to take an immediate write-off of the difference between the book value and the price of scrap. Similarly, the foundry enforced little discipline in winding up production at the end of a production run. A few leftover products were not considered a problem, as they could always be shipped at the start of the next order. It wasn't recognised as a financial problem that the next order often came almost a year later.

The formation of the joint venture gave us an opportunity to clear up a lot of that old dead inventory, but it also provided the setting for another particularly Chinese example of benighted financial management. The investment basis of the joint-venture agreement was that the Chinese partner (the Gaozhou government) would provide the land and buildings and experienced staff of the Gaozhou Foundry; the Hong Kong partner would put in an investment of cash. This agreement was signed several months before the joint venture actually took effect, and by the time I arrived on the scene I found that Mr Chow and Mr Chin had already made plans for the application of the Hong Kong partner's cash injection. They were planning to use it for new buildings, buying new equipment and undertaking renovations. Some of the contracts had already been negotiated. They explained their plans in some detail, with a sort of budget showing how all the projects could just be completed with the available funds.

After listening to their explanation I tried to bring up the subject of working capital. I pointed out that the foundry was already fully exploiting its bank lines, and that one of the stated objectives of the joint venture was to multiply the turnover of the old foundry several-fold. Certainly all this new equipment

125

would be helpful, but wouldn't we be wise to set aside some of the new cash to help finance the accelerated pace of operations? At first they didn't quite understand what I was suggesting. 'Well, what about wages?' I said. 'If we're shipping more, we're going to have to pay out a lot more per month, right? And how about freight charges? And all the subcontractors? They always need to be paid up front so they can buy their materials, right? It's just going to take a lot more of the readies to get the whole show moving faster.'

'Don't worry,' they countered. 'The bank will pay.'

'What do you mean, "the bank will pay"? We're already right up to our limits.'

'Oh, don't worry about the limits. They know you're a foreigner. We'll show them the new buildings and equipment, and they'll raise the limits. No problem.'

And that's exactly what happened. There was no quantitative discussion of return on investment. The job of the banks is to assist the government in keeping the economy working and expanding. The government decides, on whatever basis, which enterprises will be funded, and the banks implement their decisions. In this case, everyone but me understood that the local and regional authorities could never lose face by allowing their first, flagship joint venture to struggle or fail for lack of finance. Adequate finance was never in question. They could spend the Hong Kong investment like kids writing a Christmas list.

In this atmosphere you can imagine that managing the cash flow is Mr Ho's main day-to-day activity. In a conventional Chinese enterprise the Accounting Manager has little control over sales receipts, because sales are largely mandated by the plan. A claim for payment is presented through the banking system, but the actual timing of the remittance is largely in the hands of the bank. Cheques are almost unknown. If the customer has a balance of funds on deposit it's possible to be paid promptly, but only if the bank itself is not caught in a cash crunch. Usually it's very difficult to predict when money owed will be received, so the cash-management function consists of working with the bank to allocate the credit line among all the various creditors, while the bank tries to pursue its counterpart banks to bring in some of the outstanding receivables.

Export sales are even less controllable. The foundry used to book export sales only when payment was received. Everything that had been shipped and not yet paid for was carried (usually for at least three months) as work in process inventory, the reason being that the import/export agencies refused to carry exchange rate risk. They held letters of credit from the foreign customers denominated in foreign currencies, and they would place orders with the factories priced on the basis of those letters of credit and the prevailing exchange rate. But in China an import/export agency has no mechanism to hedge its foreign exchange risk, so they reserved the right to recalculate the factory's price at the exchange rate prevailing when they are finally able to cash the letter of credit. You would suppose that this should be the agency's risk, but in China the factories have no choice. If they want to export they must deal through these agencies, so the agencies make the rules. Back at the foundry, lacking any fancy techniques to deal with these contingent revenues, the book-keepers took the path of least resistance. They shipped the goods and waited a few months for the agency to remit the money. Then they wrote the invoice. Simple really, and not all that misleading. During the interim the 'work in process' was already being credited against the unit's output quota. And no one was familiar with the idea of calculating inventory turnover and tracking it as a performance measure.

This unpredictable financial system complicates running a business, but it poses even more serious problems for the hapless bureaucrats trying to manage the national economy. These days, even *laissez-faire* Hong Kong subscribes to the theory that it is government's duty to manage the economy to the benefit of the stockbrokers and the detriment of the pawnbrokers. Capitalist countries have put aside their capitalist principles to create for their central banks various levers for adjusting the supply of credit, interest rates and exchange rates in an effort to guide the economy along paths deemed appropriate by the government of the day. Paradoxically, Marxists have no ideological qualms about government management of the economy, but their dogma puts most of the effective levers out of their reach. As a result, we see supposedly capitalist Hong Kong and Taiwan managing their economies rather effectively, while the supposedly dirigiste People's Republic finds the economy not responding to orders.

The root of their problem is private property. Because China theoretically is one big centrally controlled economic machine, there is no theoretical justification for the central bank to rediscount the loan portfolios of the financial sector. This rediscounting mechanism would ration credit in favour of the projects with the highest rate of return. But without it credit is allocated at the discretion of the planners, just like any other resource. If credit is not subject to supply and demand, of course supply and demand can't help to set interest rates. High interest rates would only frustrate the planners' efforts by channelling credit to the profitable rather than the needy. Similarly, the exchange rate must be kept under the control of the planners, so the currency must be non-convertible in order to prevent the exchange rate moving in response to the outside influence of the world market. All the conventional economic levers are thus disabled, and control of the economy comes down to the basics: printing currency, direct rationing of credit on a case-by-case basis and fixing the official exchange rate.

In fact, this crude macroeconomic management coped reasonably well for three decades. It coped because China was a closed society bent on self-sufficiency. The problems arose when the leaders faced the fact that the economy was falling far behind the pace set by Japan, Korea and Taiwan and something had to be done to raise living standards a bit faster. Population control was one war front (as the Chinese would express it), and on that front the battles went rather well. But the second front consisted of modernising agriculture, technology, the military and industry. This involved co-operation and trade with other nations, and on that battle front they're starting to feel like Napoleon at the gates of Moscow.

The joint ventures have been a principal mechanism of the 'Four Modernisations'. Some of these have not worked out, but Gold Land is in many ways a typical example of those that have been successful. China has done its part in providing a factory and reasonably diligent skilled labour. The Hong Kong partner has used its freedom of travel to get out into the foreign markets and more than double the sales in the first year. They brought in new and more modern equipment, and we were able to redesign some of the management systems to make the old foundry run quite a bit more efficiently.

But joint venturers can't be paid in non-convertible currency. And they won't be tempted by unrealistic fixed exchange rates. So the government has been forced to create a parallel free market in foreign exchange. This was supposed to be restricted to joint ventures, but of course the joint ventures are not buying cheap Chinese currency to stuff a mattress. They're spending it in China, and the inevitable result has been inflation.

Down at the grass roots, Gold Land has doubled the output of the foundry and is pouring more than twice the previous monthly piecework payments into the pockets of the employees. So the new policies have raised living standards just as intended. It's too bad that the supply of goods and services hasn't doubled as well, because this has led to inflation. Inflation in a nation of subsistence farmers is not quite the same animal we know in a developed economy, but it has the effect of creating obvious economic classes to supplement China's neo-feudal class system.

So far the central planners have tried to cope in the ways they understand best—cash rationing, for example. Every business has a cash quota. It's not allowed to hoard cash, and it's only allowed to withdraw cash from the bank at a rate set by its quota. As a joint venture our quota allows us enough cash on pay day to meet our payroll, but many state-owned units have to pay part of each worker's salary with government promissory notes. Large cash payments are generally prohibited. Payments must be made by cheque (very rare around Gaozhou) or by bank transfer. Individuals are not legally compelled to keep their funds in the bank, but Chinese society can exert very heavy pressure through the party, schools and the neighbourhood committees. As you might suppose, money once deposited can be pretty hard to withdraw again.

Even joint ventures are not immune to this problem. Gold Land is profitable and generally a good credit risk, so we have no trouble securing ample credit lines. The problem comes when we try to use them. On many occasions we have been forced to write a cheque to a supplier for less than we owe. We want to pay in full, and our line of credit might contain ample funds, but we know we must co-ordinate with the bank before writing big cheques. The Gaozhou branch runs on such a thin float that if we use our full line of credit unexpectedly we can leave the branch insolvent.

Employees who deposit their wages often find that when they try to withdraw cash they're rationed to a certain maximum withdrawal because that particular branch is short of banknotes. This is particularly critical at the lunar New Year, when factories and families have the custom of giving cash gifts. The factory has to begin storing up notes months in advance to ensure that it has enough to give to all the employees.

In an effort to alleviate some of these problems the government has made payment by transfer (or by cheque) mandatory in many transactions. Of course, the local bicycle repairman will still insist on cash. He certainly has no account in which to deposit a cheque. But work units are required to settle many kinds of transactions through the bank.

In a capitalist economy this sounds like an unnecessary requirement. Why would a factory prefer to receive 100 000 yuan in currency, to the point where it must be compelled to take a bank transfer instead? The reason is that China's national monetary policy consists largely of creating credit in the banking system by the usual central planning technique of simply telling the banks what quantity of loans (and even which loans) they can write. In recent years China has had its first taste of inflation since the communist government came to power, so the government has instructed the banks to limit their loan portfolios. This controls the size of the money supply, and is probably effective in fighting inflation, but the actual working mechanism gives a rough ride to users of the banking system.

When money is scarce the banks feel the scarcity as much as anyone else. To try to conserve their own supply of funds the banks' main weapon is to delay the processing of bank transfers and cheques. Our bank, for example, receives requests for payment directly from our suppliers. The suppliers send a demand for payment through their bank directly to our bank, with only a copy to us for our information. If we disagree with the demand we have four days to object; otherwise our bank is obliged to deduct the money from our account and transfer it to our supplier without any explicit authorisation on our part.

In fact, the bank doesn't want to do so; often it doesn't even have enough funds to comply. So they collude with us in delaying, objecting and otherwise trying to bend the strict four-day payment schedule. Certain units, however, have a special priority. We don't have four days to pay our taxes or our electricity or water bills. These units are authorised to raid our accounts directly. Our only defence is to keep our account balance literally on zero. But in this, too, the bank is willing to collude if these units keep their funds in another bank, as each bank must do all it can to hoard funds and avoid transferring them out. The payments system is crippled, and that 100 000 yuan in banknotes begins to look like a useful sum to be receiving in cash.

Gold Land has one of the largest cash flows in the Gaozhou area, so we try to co-operate with the banks as best we can to help them manage their supply of funds. But this means that occasionally we have to take our share of the problems. On one occasion we had deposited some funds to pay suppliers, but when Mr Ho tried to arrange the transfer he found that half a million yuan had disappeared from our account. This couldn't have been our water bill. Enquiry revealed that the bank had been desperate for funds to repay a loan which fell due from another bank. Ours was one of the few accounts with a large balance, so they had suddenly, and without telling us, cancelled a short-term loan and seized our funds to service their own inter-bank debt.

You may be impelled to ask why the government can't absorb part of the load of economic management through taxation. Significantly, I can't tell you very much about taxes, because Gold Land doesn't pay any. When the Chinese government first considered encouraging foreign investment they took a lot of advice from Hong Kong entrepreneurs. These investors were not prepared to submit their investments to the whims of government and party functionaries, so they insisted on strong legal and contractual protection. The typical joint-venture contract provides for a zero tax rate during the first three profit-making years. This is backed up by the joint-venture legislation and regulations, and the government has been living by these agreements. As a result, the most active and successful sector of the economy, and the sector causing most of the problems with inflation, was temporarily set outside the tax net.

Units which do pay taxes are on a very simple system—they pay 5 per cent of their turnover. This is heavy taxation. A Western firm might have a 50 per cent tax rate, but the taxes are calculated only on its profits. It might make a 3 per cent profit from its operations, then have to pay half of it away in tax. A Chinese firm earning 3 per cent from its operations pays it all away, and goes into the red to pay the balance. In theory, the government could organise various rebates, exemptions and allowances to fine-tune this simple structure, but they know that in China this would immediately lead to all sorts of political pressures and influence peddling. So their scope for manoeuvre is limited.

China has an income tax on individuals which would seem much more familiar to a capitalist visitor. Nominally, there is a Western-style progressive rate structure running up to 50 per cent. The minimum threshold is 800 yuan per month. Very, very few Chinese citizens make this much income from legal employment, though it's rumoured that many officials often receive more than this in illegal payoffs. Foreign teachers and aid employees are exempted from the income tax, and in any case often receive most of their benefits in housing and so on, with a cash salary less than the threshold.

Foreign business people are subject to the tax, but most of them are from Hong Kong where they pay at a flat 16 or 17 per cent. Early in the game they convinced the Chinese government that it would be fruitless to ask Hong Kong entrepreneurs to come to China, and then try to tax them at 30 or 40 per cent. The entrepreneurs could easily manipulate their income in ways the Chinese authorities couldn't control. They could effectively decide for themselves how much tax they felt like paying. China's most effective course was to set its rate equal to Hong Kong's in order to remove the incentive for any complicated evasion schemes. So foreign employees get a 50 per cent abatement, which brings the effective rate down to about 16 per cent for most visitors. This probably does, in fact, minimise evasion and maximise China's revenue, but it prevents China from adjusting tax rates as an economic control mechanism. It would be pretty ineffective in any case. I've been paying my taxes every month for almost two years, and in all that time I've been issued receipts with consecutive serial numbers. In all of Gaozhou county I'm the only individual taxpayer.

In the West, business firms and nation states rely on their financial reports as a consistent way to keep score. China's accountants profess to be trying to perform a similar function. In China, though, the rules of the game are so confused and illogical that keeping score often seems a waste of time. As Mr Ho struggles to master the technicalities of his profession, he must find this situation most depressing.

8

One hand washes the other

IN Chinese society the extended family is a very strong social force, so it's not surprising that the ethos of the extended family carries over into business life. This is evident even in modern Hong Kong, where entrepreneurs invariably try to maintain family control of their companies. But it's even more prevalent in China, where business must work outside the official channels to get anything done. We have seen how the normal buyer/seller relationship has been distorted by the family-like concept of the relationship, and dealings with bureaucracy are even more dependent on the special access a relationship can provide. Much of the domestic propaganda work of the Communist Party is devoted to developing a sense of public spirit and the public good, which goes against the extended family tradition. But personal contacts remain the key to getting things done. There is little tradition of the professional bureaucrat whose job it is to treat all applicants fairly according to published rules. China relies instead on a system of contacts and relationships akin to the extended family to set priorities and allocate scarce resources. This system is also very strong in South America, in most African countries, as well as in Italy and Japan. By contrast the 'faceless bureaucracy', which was created to distribute government services on an impartial and impersonal basis, free from individual influence and family ties, works well in places like northern Europe and North America. But the Chinese, and

134

other family-oriented societies, find this a strange and uncomfortable way to get things done. It's a bit like shopping in a supermarket instead of bargaining in a street market; they can live with it if they have to, but they would rather not.

In rural China you can occasionally see a religious official in full, traditional regalia conducting rites to open a new building. Even today, even in the countryside, this is a violation of socialist principles and is officially discouraged. Few party members would dare openly to consult a geomancer or astrologer about siting or inaugurating his new house. A party member would normally be obliged to set an example by belittling the whole process, at least in public. But he would not, of course, be able to follow the party line in arranging the site, the builder, the materials and the various government approvals necessary. Solving these problems requires contacts, friends and influence. Using contacts, friends and influence for private ends is an extreme violation of socialist principles, but here the party is an accessory to the crime. Party members are the first in line as new home owners, primarily because they are party members. The party itself is a principal source of the friends, contacts and influence they need to negotiate the house-building process. The party itself is the instrument for breaking the rules. But in this case the party is only taking over some of the role that, in China, has traditionally been filled by the extended family. 'The party is my family,' the revolutionaries say. In China this is part of the problem.

Most Westerners who have visited China as independent tourists would say that there are two ways to travel: the hard way and the easy way. The easy way involves buying your transportation through uncrowded ticketing agencies, travelling first class and staying in modern Hong Kong-managed hotels. The hard way is the backpacker's familiar saga of interminable queues, standing for sixteen hours in a packed railroad car, unsanitary food, unsavoury accommodation and a daily dose of surly or disdainful 'service'.

In fact, the Chinese are not familiar with either of these two approaches. A Chinese travelling for business or for any other reason will always try to arrange his trip within the network of his contacts. The core of these contacts is, of course, his extended family. But this core is expanded to include business acquaintances, old schoolmates, army comrades, the families of all of these, their friends, and families of friends of friends. A Chinese who needs to travel will go to almost any lengths to expand his circle of contacts wide enough that he can stay within it throughout the journey.

It's occasionally necessary for one of our staff to travel to Guangzhou, the provincial capital. This is a twelve-hour road journey. There is no train, plane or boat. The most comfortable transportation is the night bus, which has reserved seats, air-conditioning and videotapes for diversion. It remains a twelve-hour bus trip, but it's a big improvement on the alternatives. The company can extend the network at our end of the line because a relative of one of our employees is employed at the local bus station. So there's no need to line up for the tickets; we simply tell our contact in advance and he buys them for us. At the Guangzhou end of the trip the joint venture maintains an office with a dormitory and kitchenette. So at any time of day or night the company traveller (or sometimes one of his family, friends or schoolmates) immediately has a *pied à terre* where he can get in off the street, safe within his net of relationships. There's no need to seek out a hotel, fill out forms or deal with surly hotel staff.

Nevertheless, some of our staff, even senior managers, prefer to travel to Guangzhou in the trucks we use to ship our merchandise. This trip is much longer and rougher, and there is no air-conditioning, video or even a radio. They don't do this to save money—the company pays for business travel. They prefer to travel by truck because the truckers are local people who, at least in a distant sense, can be called friends of a friend of a friend. The truck leaves directly from our factory and delivers the traveller to the door of our Guangzhou office, so no matter what calamity may befall him the traveller is within his net of contacts all the way. There is no need to deal as a stranger with so much as a taxi-driver or a waitress.

This approach is available to the foreign traveller as well. It's called the guided tour. Foreign visitors ascribe all sorts of sinister motives to the Chinese attempts to arrange tours for them. There may be underlying motives to some extent, but beneath it all the Chinese simply don't understand why Westerners would choose to deal with the hostile world as an independent traveller. If they could read the books written about China written by Western travellers they would be confirmed in their doubts. The Chinese themselves have no time or money for touring. But the tour is the Chinese way of offering the visitor a surrogate for the web of contacts which, for the Chinese, is a vital element of social existence.

The average Chinese lives his daily life within a stable routine. For long periods, or even throughout his entire life, he sees the same family, workmates and neighbours in the same situations every day. The typical Chinese has one job with the same employer throughout his career. He rarely travels or has any sort of holiday; only occasionally would he even go shopping. The average Chinese, after all, lives in a village and trades produce with his neighbours. Even the factory employee works six days a week, lives in his factory and eats from the factory canteen. Within this daily round he feels and is secure.

But from time to time everyone is compelled (in the West we might say 'has the opportunity') to step outside the daily routine. People get sick, they get married, they want to buy a radio or a new pair of shoes. At these moments the challenge for the Chinese is to negotiate this disruption as painlessly as possible, and normally this can best be accomplished by using his contacts.

If necessary, a Chinese in need of a pair of shoes can go to the shop and ask the clerk to let him try on the various styles available at the moment. If he finds something he likes and has the cash, he can pay for his purchase and carry it home on his bicycle. But in fact he will probably find the styles and quality unsatisfactory and/or his size unavailable. He would perhaps have to visit stores in various towns over a wide area (a practical impossibility) to find a style he likes. He may have to go through twenty pairs to find one free of defects. He may have to wait through several stock replenishments before he finds something really suitable. All in all, it will be much preferable if he can identify a contact in a shop or in the shoe industry who can give him a hand. Nothing too onerous. Just keep an eye on the new shipments, put aside something he might like and perhaps give him a discount.

As with shoes, so with a husband. Of course, in principle, a young girl can quite respectably develop friendships among her acquaintances. Less respectably, she can attend the movies or even the dances that are starting to appear in some towns. But all in all she'll probably be much better served by relying on her family and their vast web of contacts to arrange something for her.

And of course it's occasionally necessary to apply for a bicycle licence, to have plumbing installed, to seek medical care or to reserve a desirable work or school place. On these important occasions, how best to proceed? It goes without saying . . .

It's hard to say whether the chicken comes before the egg. The man who allocates the school places is a man like any other. When he needs a bicycle licence he looks to his network; and he must expect the bicycle licence man to do the same. Each official, then, is fed a daily diet of requests for precedence and preferential treatment. Virtually everyone who submits an application has, it seems, dredged up some grounds, however far-fetched, for requesting some sort of priority consideration. The normal official channels of application become disused, and the service offered through the normal channels is not a matter of much concern. Nevertheless, the official has a desk which he is expected to man for at least a certain period every day. And sitting at his desk leaves him open to the entreaties of one more class of supplicant: poor souls such as foreign visitors who for some reason have not been able to establish a 'valid' claim to priority service.

In this situation what is service? What is priority? What is a claim? This is when the outsider must, by the logic of the system, offer a packet of cigarettes, some banknotes or a visa for study in America to claim his place (or is it someone else's place?) in the 'queue'. In this situation it's a bit difficult to buy even a train ticket without connections.

The situation is supposed to be repugnant to state socialism, but the very powerful state has never been able to do much about it. Perhaps, in fact, a powerless state would be more successful. In any case, it's not clear that Western moral repugnance has much relevance one way or the other. Your best move is to take the guided tour.

Chinese work units and Chinese individuals avoid these problems, to a large extent, by devoting a great deal of their time and energy to cultivating their acquaintances and building up debts of mutual obligation. Because China attempts to operate as a totalitarian state, the preponderance of these efforts is directed towards various government and party organisations and office-holders. It would be incorrect to imagine, however, that this cultivation normally takes the form of bribes and kickbacks. These are the most visible surface layer, but the really effective efforts operate on a much deeper and longer-term basis.

Our joint venture, for example, is one of about 45 major manufacturing enterprises in the county. Like the others, we must maintain almost daily contact with the town's senior leaders and the leaders of the major government departments. Ostensibly, Gold Land appointed a Western General Manager to upgrade the factory's efficiency, but the managers of the foundry and the leaders of the government welcome me for quite a different reason. As the only Caucasian living in the area my presence in their town brings them 'face' (prestige) in their dealings with their circle of contacts. Many of the steady stream of visitors who arrive to 'study our situation' have in fact been invited by local government officials who want to show off 'their' Western manager. By receiving these visitors, and entertaining them at some expense, Gold Land weaves another thread or two into the tapestry of its relationship with whatever government or party organ issued the invitation.

This steady trickle of visitors has enabled me, in just a couple of years, to build up a collection of business cards that most Chinese managers would build and maintain over a whole career. In a country where so much of the population is functionally illiterate and where paper is so expensive, it may seem surprising that the business card is such a pervasive business tool. In fact, there are some interesting circumstances which make business cards vital, not just in business but in most activities of the upper social classes.

The businessman in China goes through a lot of calling cards—particularly the Western businessman, as he and his business contacts find each other's names difficult to pronounce and impossible to remember. 'Purves' is in some ways particularly nasty, as the 'r'and 'v' are invariably pronounced as 'l' and 'w' by all but the best English speakers. So I adopted a Chinese name early on and use it universally. In fact, I adopted my Chinese name on the occasion of my 40th birthday. On the principle that life begins at 40 I consulted some friends and colleagues, and two of the secretaries in the office came up with the name I now use daily.

Chinese names are complicated by some peculiarities of the language. Each of the Chinese dialects has about as many sounds as other common languages, but they use them in an inefficient way. The Chinese language tries to express each concept in a word of only one or two syllables. This limitation drastically reduces the number of allowable words, so in speech each allowable word must serve to express several quite different concepts. In writing, on the other hand, each concept can be written with its own unique ideogram. The result is that it's easy to compile lists of ideograms which don't look at all similar and express unrelated concepts, yet which all have identical pronunciation. It's just like homophones in English, but English homophones are rare.

Personal names in Chinese usually consist of three syllables, to distinguish them from normal words. Each syllable is represented in writing by one Chinese character. Having selected three allowable sounds which roughly render the sounds of my English name into the Cantonese dialect, the next step was to check that in speech the three sounds couldn't be pronounced so as to mean 'such a fool' or something even less desirable. Then came the process of selecting from the many possible characters used for writing each of the three sounds. Normally this should be a matter of high culture, but in my case it was necessary to select simple characters which I could learn to write reasonably legibly and not render as 'dirty dishonest thief' by mistake. In fact, my colleagues seem to have chosen my name wisely. I eventually learned to write it without sneaking a look at my business card, and I have even received the odd compliment on it as a particularly cultured choice. The selection took about a week.

But, of course, Chinese businessmen—as well as teachers, students and anyone with a claim to some sort of job title—don't carry business cards just to exchange with foreigners. The point of it all is that most of the one-billion-plus Chinese all share just a hundred or so family names. Most Chinese can rhyme off the list of the ten most popular (the current leader is known in English as Lee), as well as the ranking of their own name. First names seem, if anything, to be even more limited. Many adults have names like 'Love China' and 'Support Mao', but children are now being named 'Little Orchid' and 'Strong Loyal' in the classical way. When China reaches the point of installing personal telephone lines, this extreme paucity of names is going to pose an interesting problem for whoever is assigned to compile the telephone directory. And addresses won't be of any help in solving this problem. The 800 people who live in the factory at Gold Land all have the same address!

Another confusing factor when learning Chinese names is the lack of a single, common language. China is still divided into hundreds of distinct linguistic regions. Most Chinese business is done in Guangdong Province and/or Hong Kong, where the dialect spoken is Cantonese. Beijing is probably next, where they speak something pretty close to the national language, Putonghua (literally 'common speech'). Third is Shanghai, which has a third, quite distinct, dialect. These dialects are about as similar as French, Spanish and Italian.

Foreign linguists have devised various systems for rendering each dialect into roman letters (and Cyrillic ones too, for that matter), but none of these systems applies to all the dialects. In any case, the Chinese don't know these systems any more than you know the Chinese systems for rendering English words into Chinese characters. Nevertheless, a Chinese businessman will ordinarily have a go at printing his name and address in roman letters on the back of his business card. The only system for doing so that his printer is likely to know is the official Pinyin system for writing the Putonghua dialect in roman letters. So although the businessman himself may speak no Putonghua, his printer transliterates the Putonghua pronunciation of his name.

I first stubbed my toe on this common practice when I met a Cantonese fellow who had spent five years at Texas Tech. He dusted off his rusty English and introduced himself as Ng Geen Guy. No problem there. 'How do you do.' Except that he then proffered a name card which clearly read on the reverse side, 'Wu Jie Jee'. Huh? Here's how it works.

Ng is one of the one hundred or so common family names and is very popular in the Cantonese-speaking parts of the country. It's written in Chinese with a particular Chinese character. Many people in other parts of the country also write their names with that same character, but they pronounce it differently depending on the local dialect. In areas where Putonghua is spoken, Mr Ng's character is pronounced 'Wu', so that's how his character is represented in Pinyin, and that's what his printer put on the 'English' side of his name card. The same distortion was applied to his other two name characters. 'Geen' and 'Guy' became 'Jie' and 'Jee'. If Mr Ng and I could both speak Putonghua, of course, I could call him Mr Wu and all would be well. In fact, his name card was initially more confusing than helpful.

Addresses are less contentious, but even the addresses on business cards are not without their problems. Computer typesetting is unknown in China. The little local printshops that do name cards print by the old-fashioned method of setting lead type letter by letter. In Chinese this is quite a trick, as there are thousands of commonly used characters, so setting any important document involves rummaging around for a few of the characters among a vast inventory of type. But name cards are much simpler. Names and addresses use the same characters over and over again, so the Chinese side of most name cards is set to a high standard.

Unfortunately, foreign visitors tend to be more interested in the side with roman lettering, and on that side the quality of the typesetting immediately falls to pieces. It should be easier to get it right with only 26 letters and 10 digits to choose from, but in a small place like Gaozhou the typesetter is likely to be rather weak in Putonghua. He can tell an 'A' from a 'B', but may often set 'm' by using an upside down 'w'. Or a comma might be set by using an inverted apostrophe. The result is a very ragged line of type indeed, with letters bouncing up and down through the words and erratic spacing. Furthermore, the typesetters have no real appreciation of the different **typefaces** used with roman letters, so the same letter may appear in large and small type, **bold** and *italic*, all within the same line of type. Once their type stocks are pied, they can't discriminate well enough to sort them out again.

This seems to be a difficult problem to avoid in China. You might expect it in a little country town like Gaozhou, but even visiting bigwigs from Guangzhou, the most modern and technically advanced city in China, present name cards showing the same problems. One of Gold Land's primary objectives is to earn foreign exchange, so we try not to waste it by importing supplies from outside China. Nevertheless, after several attempts to train some of our local printers we have had to arrange for our business cards to be printed in Hong Kong. Most of our guests don't have access to this solution, so when trading business cards in the courtyard I often have to swallow hard to suppress a chuckle at what I'm reading.

It is important to keep a well-organised file of these cards, however, because having entertained a visitor the relationship is established to the point where I can then call on him for assistance should the need arise. I once spent a pleasant afternoon in this cause entertaining a young lady known as 'The Princess' because she's the daughter of the mayor. The mayor thought she would enjoy spending an afternoon hanging about my office and could at the same time practise her English. I doubt that she found an afternoon of my mega-meeting very interesting, but I was happy enough to welcome her, as this is a unique service that our factory can provide to government officials. It in turn means that we can call on them for unique kinds of support or for preference over other work units.

On one occasion, for example, we found that some employees who had left the Gaozhou Foundry to try private business were giving up and returning to work for some of the small foundries in the area. As we were in need of their skills we explained the problem to one of our government contacts who offered to prohibit these other units from 'stealing our workers'. On other

143

occasions a senior party official has instructed the bank to allocate scarce credit to our factory; not, of course, on the basis of any financial analysis of our needs, but on the basis of our requests, his various obligations to us, and the overriding fundamental postulate that this high-visibility enterprise with the Canadian manager must be given every possible assistance. Unfortunately for the Chinese economy, much of the credit rationing seems to be conducted on such bases. Our joint venture is only one tiny example of this very serious problem.

On the other hand, a good relationship with the mayor is not a key to the city. The mayor too works through his contacts, and where his contacts are weak he too must defer to established relationships. Those who have laid their groundwork step in ahead of him for service. This was illustrated one day when we were reviewing our safety programme.

The managers had been making various proposals for safety improvements. 'But what about the traffic accidents?' I asked. All of their proposals had dealt with factory operations, when in fact our most frequent and serious accidents were traffic accidents involving our vehicles. 'It doesn't matter,' they said. 'Well, I don't know,' I persisted. 'It seems to me that in the last few months we've had a lot more people injured out on the highways than in the workshops. And when they find out that our driver works for a foreign joint venture, those highway casualties are the guys who are likely to cause us trouble. Sooner or later we're going to knock down someone whose brother is a magistrate.' 'That's Joe Lee's programme,' they countered. (Mr Lee Jo Yau is our Shipping Manager.) 'Really? I haven't heard of any programme.' 'But General Manager,' they explained, 'Joe Lee has excellent relations with the Traffic Bureau.'

I eventually realised that proposals about traffic safety would not interest the body we were currently addressing. In fact, the purpose of our meeting was not primarily to improve safety conditions at all. It was to draft a document on the subject of safety which the government Safety Bureau could tabulate among its achievements of the current plan year. Through subsequent observation I realised that the company was maintaining two relationships in this field. One set of dinners, cigarettes and other favours was managed by our Safety Officer; the other was directed at another bureaucracy and managed by Joe Lee, the Shipping Manager. Both were being prepared against the day when we would have an accident in one or the other realm and would have to call on our relationships to counter whatever relationships the injured party could bring to bear on the case.

Whether it's purchasing, selling, finance or motivating the workforce, in China business success is above all a question of relationships. It would be a mistake to imagine that these relationships are cemented primarily by under-the-table payments. On the contrary, illicit payments are the desperate expedient of the passenger without a relationship who wants to secure a sleeping berth on the crowded train. The regular passengers on the run are the ones who have the relationships. They've been sharing their cigarettes and the odd bottle of beer with the conductor every time they've ridden this run for weeks, months or even years. They may well have bought him dinner once or twice. They have no need to pass him folded banknotes now. They can relax, confident that the relationship they need today has been prepared well in advance.

A well-run Chinese work unit cultivates its relationships with exactly the same foresight. Apart from a long series of conventional business dealings there are two constant relationship-building procedures. One is mutual visits, which we'll examine in due course. The other is banqueting. Good-quality gifts can be hard to find in China, but every town has one or two spots that will turn out a very acceptable banquet.

Tourists return with a whole album of memories of China, but businessmen normally remember the banquets. As in few other cultures, banquets in China are part of the backbone of a strong business relationship. Fortunately, Westerners almost invariably find the Chinese banquet a thoroughly enjoyable experience. The various Chinese cuisines are, after all, among the world's best. And long experience has taught Chinese businessmen how to make the banquet an animated and convivial event. The only complaint of most visiting businessmen is that the banquets are too frequent. On a tour of Chinese suppliers or customers most Westerners are expected to enjoy two or even three banquets a

145

day. Even the most enthusiastic lover of Chinese food quickly finds this to be too much of a good thing. Government officials and Hong Kong businessmen who spend much of their time in China normally have what for the Chinese is an entirely uncharacteristic weight problem.

Banqueting is essential to relationship-building. A basic reason for this is that very few Chinese executives have an office they can feel proud of. Even the Factory Director often works from a drab and ill-lit cubbyhole, and usually he shares his office with others of his staff. A long lunch in a spacious and air-conditioned restaurant is a welcome diversion. Another factor is that personal chemistry is considered a vital part of every business relationship. Price, terms, reliability and quality are all part of the agreement. But beyond all that, the Chinese businessman feels a cultural need to base his business dealings on a bond of friendship. In a planned economy this friendship is often the real basis of the deal. But even in a modern market setting the Chinese businessman feels uneasy about dealing with someone he doesn't also like and respect as a person. Sadly, this often leads on to hypocrisy, with business associates glad-handing and feigning undying friendships with persons they neither like nor respect.

Finally, it's worth remembering that even the most prosperous managers of the new China have personally experienced suffering and privation in the recent past. Like the generation of American businessmen who survived the dirty 'thirties, Chinese managers remember the years of the Cultural Revolution. Even today they appreciate a good meal for its own sake. They have no yachts, corporate jets or luxurious houses. At home they usually eat peasant-style, with a huge basin of rice garnished with a small helping of stewed meat and vegetables. For all these reasons, banqueting remains a central perk of Chinese business.

In England or America many towns lack even a single decent restaurant. In Germany or Switzerland you'll not likely get a bad meal, but many restaurants fail to rise above a certain level of mediocrity. Fortunately, southern China can better be compared with France, Italy or Japan, where quality is a uniform preoccupation. Even the backpacking tourist can attest that in Guangdong Province it's difficult to find a bad meal. Even the poorest greasy-chopstick or tarpaper roadside stall serves meals which, though simple, are nevertheless prepared with care and taste delicious.

A Westerner is invariably invited to the best restaurant in town. Among the Chinese themselves, the class of restaurant is a reliable guide to the status of the visitor. Somewhat impatient with the entire expensive charade, I (to the despair of my staff) sometimes invite visitors to eat in our factory (where the guesthouse food is in fact quite good) or at a small eating stall across the road from the factory gate. This uncivilised behaviour should bring me a loss of face. It can be overlooked only because I'm a barbarous foreigner who doesn't understand the niceties of Chinese business etiquette.

Most good restaurants have one or two large central rooms surrounded by smaller private rooms, each large enough for just two tables. These smaller rooms are the usual venue for business meals, both for reasons of status and to provide privacy for the serious discussions that the Chinese normally expect to conduct while eating.

The Chinese dining table is round. Platters of food are traditionally placed in the centre, and each diner serves himself one morsel at a time from the central supply. The diameter of the table is just large enough that an adult can reach slightly beyond the centre without rising from his chair. This standard diameter will just accommodate twelve diners comfortably around the outside, so twelve is the normal 'table' for a Chinese banquet, and restaurants often offer one or two set meals designed for this number. The usual rule of thumb is to order one dish for each member of the party. With a table of twelve this offers lots of variety and is the source of the traditional Chinese twelve-course banquet.

On approaching the table the first order of business is to choose a seat. There's not much in it, except that with a full table the waitress will have to squeeze into the circle to serve. There's plenty of serving to come, so I try to sit on the side of the table furthest from the kitchen. Whichever seat I choose, as the foreigner I'm normally the honoured guest who got everyone out of the office, so it will be incumbent on the host to sit next to me where he can refill my glass and place choice morsels in my bowl from the central platter. After that there's no particular pecking order, and the other seats fill at random.

Proceedings start with cigarettes and tea. The members of the party vie with one another to produce packets of expensive imported cigarettes, which they offer around and light with a clever and/or expensive lighter. The waitress, meanwhile, will try to deduce which of us is the host by posing the innocent question, 'What kind of tea?'.

After dozens of Chinese banquets I still can claim no real grasp of the vast range of China's regional tea specialities. In the West many of us drink tea daily without ever deviating from supermarket teabags. The Chinese, however, approach their teas as the French approach their wines. Any establishment that calls itself a real restaurant must offer a selection of at least three or four varieties. If there are more than six or eight diners at the table it's not uncommon to order pots of two different types simultaneously.

Service in Chinese restaurants is normally very attentive, and the tea is brought quickly, almost before all the cigarettes are lit. The waitress pours the first round and immediately adds water to the pot. This first cup is a little appetiser, consumed while the host considers the menu. As the cups are drained, now and throughout the meal, the person seeking a refill traditionally hefts the pot and pours around to all the others first before refilling his own cup. This requires fine judgement, as filling all the other cups to the brim will usually leave the pourer, the one who wanted tea in the first place, with not enough left for himself. Recognising that this is primarily a polite ritual, the trick is to pour just a token amount into the cup of anyone who doesn't actively evidence profound thirst, leaving enough to fill your own cup full. This will pretty well drain the pot, so the pourer replaces the pot on the table but opens the lid to attract the attention of the waitress who brings more water. The waitress expects to visit each table every ten minutes or so for this purpose. So by the time the next diner discovers he has emptied his cup the next pot has steeped.

It's perfectly possible to drink only tea throughout the meal, and at lunch even foundry employees sometimes exercise this degree of self-discipline. The hosts, though, invariably insist on beer, soft-drinks and rice spirits. So before the first course is served the waitress removes the teapot and all the cups. These will return only after the last course has been eaten, when the host contemplates the bill.

Cigarettes continue throughout, though even the compulsive Chinese smokers recognise the difficulty of literally smoking and eating simultaneously. Instead, there is normally a pause between courses somewhere in mid-meal, just long enough for everyone to go through the offering-around ritual and to smoke one cigarette.

The tea pre-course is often accompanied by small dishes of appetisers. These are not to be missed, as they often feature unusual regional specialities. Peanuts and pickled onions are the basic appetisers in Guangdong restaurants, but they are often supplemented by preserved eggs, beef jerky and all sorts of other strange, but usually very tasty, tidbits. Unlike the tea, they are left on the table but are never replenished. If you should wander into a Cantonese restaurant, sit down, then change your mind and decide to go elsewhere, you will be presented with a bill for your 'place setting' which covers these appetisers.

The long, long menu typical of Chinese restaurants everywhere is entirely authentic. In China as well, large restaurants offer dozens of dishes. Ordering by consensus is impractical, so the waitress won't give you the chance. She brings one menu, hands it to the host and expects him to choose a balanced menu fitting the tastes and pocket of the group. Taste is not in fact the problem, as everyone gets to pick and choose from among all the dishes. The trick is rather to choose a balanced selection of soup, vegetable, meat and seafood dishes. To the Western eye this seems like standard menu selection, but in fact the host is heavily influenced by the Taoist theory of yin and yang—the hot and cool, male and female principles which must be balanced to make what a Chinese diner considers a rounded and healthy meal. This is why there may be a certain Alphonse and Gaston routine over who will make up the order. It's a minor cultural test. Some Westerners aspire to master the art of ordering in this

149

way, but I figure I'd only be holding myself up for ridicule. In my experience, no matter how many times you observe this process the rules, not to mention the principles behind them, remain elusive.

The beer and spirits arrive with the first course, and thus begin the drinking games. They take all the usual forms—drinking songs, challenges, boasting—all designed to inebriate the opposition without succumbing oneself. The Chinese tend to get red in the face with only a little alcohol, which makes the contest that much more fun.

The whole process is abetted by the system for serving beverages in a Chinese restaurant. After asking the diners what they intend to drink, the waitress brings several bottles and pours each diner a glass of whichever beverage he has selected. Throughout the meal she refills the glasses regularly, without ever letting them become empty, and leaves the empty bottles on a side table to tally what has been drunk, but not by whom. As a sideshow to their drinking rivalry, the diners collectively take a certain pride in their total collection of empties.

Most Western visitors try to evade these drinking bouts, but I've noticed that among our business visitors the Americans seem the most able (or willing) to enter into the spirit of the occasion. Among the Chinese, women normally avoid being drawn in, though in a foundry you can find exceptions to this rule. The only other group that often manages to evade these drinking contests is government officials. They attend a lot of banquets, and it's a genuine mark of their relative sophistication that they both eat and drink moderately. To the common businessman these banquets are one of the most important developments of the new open economic policies, and he's not about to pass up any chance to enjoy one.

In a really first-class establishment a waitress will wait at the table to serve all of the food from the central platters into the bowls, but in most places this is limited to the soup course. After that, the successive platters are simply placed in the centre of the table and the diners help themselves one or two bites at a time. Ideally, the platters are served a bit faster than they can be eaten, so that a pile of half-consumed platters accumulates in the middle of the table. By the end of the meal two or three of the earliest and best dishes may have been completely consumed and the platters removed. But there should be a mound of six to ten platters left in the centre to demonstrate that there has been an abundance of food and no one was left hungry. It's gross excess, as the Chinese government constantly emphasises in its campaigns against waste, but the symbolism is important to people who have recently known real hunger.

In the Cantonese dialect the expression 'to eat' is literally spoken as 'to eat rice'. Rice is the staple in south China, and virtually every meal, every day consists of rice garnished with some sort of meat and vegetable preparation. The rice is a heaped basinful; the garnish would barely fill a saucer. Rice (in other parts of China it would be noodles or steamed bread) is still the centrepiece of the meal to a far greater extent than bread and potatoes are in the Western diet. The business banquet is set apart as a special occasion by the fact that it includes little rice. A really good banquet includes none at all until the last course, which may be fried rice, fried noodles, steamed buns or rice porridge. At a more modest banquet there may be an order for rice earlier on. This takes the form of a call, 'Who wants rice?' and a show of hands. In contrast to everything else, the rice arrives in individual bowls. Most people eat it as one chopstick-load of rice followed immediately by a morsel from one of the platters.

Chinese cuisine is generally delicious, but most Western visitors find that they enjoy it better if they follow a cardinal rule: if you don't recognise it, don't ask. Many Chinese dishes have poetic names along the lines of 'Love Nest of the Dragon and the Phoenix'. But most Chinese can no more render this poetry into English than you could render 'Hawaiian Pizza' into Chinese. So instead they tell you, truthfully, that this is a very special dish made from the penises of five different endangered species. Interesting, but better appreciated after the meal.

Unfortunately, there is no such simple rule for adapting to Chinese table manners. After many years in China and Hong Kong I still find this one of the least attractive aspects of Chinese culture. It's only small consolation to realise that conventional

151

Chinese table manners agree pretty well with those current in most parts of the world and that Euro-American norms are in fact a minority cult. Be prepared, then, for plenty of chewing with the mouth open, speaking with the mouth full, belching at the table, and particularly extroverted slurping of soup and rice porridge. Unfortunately, rice porridge is a morning staple, and many visitors find this egregious violation of Western conventions particularly hard to bear in the early morning. Spitting bones on the table is, by comparison, a minor peccadillo.

Most banquets end rather abruptly. The diners slow, and finally admit defeat in the face of the mound of still partly laden platters covering the table. Leaving food on the platters is considered important to the success of the meal, but leaving liquor undrunk is not. So normally there's a clean-up round of toasts with 'bottoms up' strictly enforced to drain any opened bottles.

There is also a call for the waitress to bring plastic bags into which the uneaten contents of the platters are decanted to be enjoyed by the folks at home. If lower-level government employees are hosting the banquet, two or three fresh platters of particularly choice dishes may arrive at this time. These supplements, which have been ordered especially for home consumption, can be slipped on to the bill and carried home in their entirety. It's embarrassing to watch this charade, but for government agency employees it has, unfortunately, become accepted practice.

But if you're lucky you won't be dining with bureaucrats. You'll be hosted by the hard-drinking employees of a cast iron foundry. If that's the case, when the eating is done the singing begins. Having studied singing in school doesn't ensure that they sing well, but it does ensure that they know lots of songs and are relatively uninhibited about singing them in public. If the occasion is the least bit special, and particularly if there are at least two tables participating, Gold Land banquets often conclude with an hour or two of singing. Needless to say, this takes some of our foreign guests by surprise. I recall one German who was reduced to singing 'O Tannenbaum' in June, as it was about the only song to which he could be certain of remembering the words. Forewarned, I've been known to organise cabaret versions of 'Honey Bun', 'The Sheik of Araby' and selected arias from Chinese operas. The singing is of course accompanied by lots more drinking, which is part of its attraction. If this were Holland no one would ever get home. Fortunately, Chinese restaurants close at around 11.00 p.m.

This relationship-building is a never-ending preoccupation of anyone associating with the Chinese. Western businessmen returning from their first visits are usually disappointed that not much else has been accomplished. With more experience they come to realise that investing in relationships is an effective way to get things done in Chinese society. The problems arise primarily when relationships lead on into outright corruption. It's a slippery slope, and it takes considerable agility to stop your slide short of the borderline.

9

A royal progress

B USINESS travel, like so much else in China, is at once a source of frustration and of delight. The Chinese worker is normally assigned to his work unit for life and, until recently, travel was severely restricted by an internal passport system. So for the average worker or manager the chance to travel represents an occasional bonus worth looking forward to.

In China it's the Purchasing Department's buyers who do most of the business travel, though their travel tends to be of a very stationary sort. Much less frequent, but much more fun, is a junket with the General Manager.

Every once in a while there is a new product, a new supplier or a new customer requiring some in-depth problem-solving or relationship-building that a buyer can't provide. There's no fax. The telephone is virtually useless. So if it can't all be arranged by letter a meeting is called for. Since we need a meeting it makes sense for me to invoke my special attraction as a foreign visitor by gracing the other work unit with a visit and accepting their hospitality. This decision taken, the word quickly spreads that one of the air-conditioned vehicles will be heading off on a trip. There will be new sights to see, unaccustomed adventures and plenty of banqueting. With a foreigner along everything will be first class, so people immediately begin scheming for a seat in the party.

We couldn't normally consider going by plane. Even when

travelling between the south coast province of Guangdong and Beijing, near the border of Inner Mongolia, most people take the train, and it's not just a case of saving money. In the first place, China has little in the way of travel agents. All domestic air travel is monopolised by a cartel of domestic airlines, so on any one route there's no competition. Only the airline writes tickets, and tickets for a particular flight are written only in the departure city. There are no round-trips. This means that plane flights can only be booked by visiting the airline office in the departure city and paying cash. China Travel Service and several other government travel bureaux will do this for you if you have some relationship which qualifies you to use their service. But most work units don't have the necessary relationship with an organisation of this kind, and they must turn instead to some other contact in the departure city.

Gaozhou, of course, has no airport. So if, for some reason, I wanted to fly to Beijing, I would first have to drive for twelve hours to Guangzhou and take a flight from there. In order to get a seat I would have to cable someone in Guangzhou who could go around to the airline office and buy me a ticket. That's not a problem in Guangzhou, where Gold Land maintains an office, but in any other city (for the return flight, for example) we would have to rely on a supplier, a customer or someone else with whom we have a relationship. He'll normally be happy to help us, as it helps cement the relationship. But we would have to suggest a range of dates, and he would cable back and inform us what he was able to get.

So far so good, but better hope we don't have to change our plans. The airlines will change a reservation, but our contact will have to send someone back to the office to do it. And if we should have to cancel our trip we'll have to take the ticket in person to the original office for a refund, and they'll deduct perhaps 50 per cent as a service fee.

For trips we make regularly, particularly if it's from a small airport where the airline has very few staff, we can alleviate these problems by the usual Chinese method of developing a relationship. Most of my trips originate from a small airport in Zhanjiang, 125 km from the factory. I sent one of the staff to buy the ticket the first few times. The staffer passed his business card to the airport manager along with some cigarettes and told her the whole story about his foreign General Manager's stay in China, flying out to Hong Kong to see his wife and so on. Now it's possible to call the manager directly and reserve a ticket to be paid for on arriving at the airport just before the flight.

If you observe the timetable you don't often miss one of these flights. They're usually late. China has a fair network of small regional airports, but many of them don't have so much as a hangar. The domestic airlines each have a regional base, and the schedules are arranged to bring all the planes back to base each night after an out-and-back hopscotch. A plane leaves the base in the morning and calls at a series of small places on the way to another major city. It then turns around and runs the route in reverse, arriving back at the base at night for maintenance. But the smaller airports have no instrument landing systems, and with all the coal that's burned in China the mornings are often foggy, particularly in winter. So although a plane may be scheduled to leave the base city at 6.00 a.m. it waits for a telex from the first stop to confirm that the visibility is suitable for landing. If it's not, the whole day's schedule is delayed. So passengers spend a lot of time waiting.

Once you've managed to get airborne the flight seems unexpectedly long, as there isn't much in the way of in-flight entertainment. No music, no film and, in a totalitarian state, no magazines. This gives you time to consider what to do with your present. The Chinese airlines customarily give each passenger a little something—a fan, perhaps, or a tie pin—as a souvenir. For most Chinese an air journey would be a once-in-a-lifetime experience, so the gift does in fact make a nice souvenir. He might even buy a tie to show off his pin. But if you do a lot of travelling you soon run out of people to give these things to. Puzzling over your next act of largesse helps to pass the time.

On arriving at your destination one of the first considerations must be reserving a ticket out again. This applies equally to planes, trains, boats and even buses. Since plane reservations open one month before the flight we ask our contact at the destination to organise this for us. If he's had any difficulty I'll have to take it in hand on arrival. If he hasn't, he'll want his money.

International travel is, in most respects, somewhat easier. In the first place, there's a choice of airlines. I make it a practice always to buy a round-trip ticket outside China with a confirmed return reservation. This eliminates all the reservation and ticketing problems, and I need only make one phone call two or three days before the flight to reconfirm. Most international flights leave from Beijing and Shanghai, but you can fly to various cities in Southeast Asia from Guangzhou and Kunming, and you can fly to Hong Kong from a large number of smaller Chinese cities. The big airports have proper instruments, so the flights are likely to leave on time. The Beijing connections to Europe can even be relatively fast, as some of the airlines have permission to fly a proper great circle over Russia, greatly reducing the distance compared to flying from Hong Kong. The main drawback is that the major airports take security relatively seriously. The nicest part of flying in south China is being able to sit out under the palm trees when your flight is delayed.

But for most journeys, plane travel is out of the question. Either one end or other of the journey is out of reach of an airport, or there's no direct flight. For these reasons most Chinese business travel is by train.

China's rail network is extensive; the schedules, if you can find out about them, are well designed; and the trains run on time. Train travel itself is often rather pleasant. Apart from the time it takes to cover long distances the main problem is, again, getting the tickets.

One bit of modern Chinese technology that I've managed to introduce to Gold Land is the All China Railway Timetable. This is published annually by the China Railway Publishing House in Beijing, but I've never seen it in China. I buy one (or two or three) of each new edition in Hong Kong, and figure I'm importing a valuable tool.

China operates three sorts of trains. If you're bound for North Korea you can sample an International Express. I never have. Then there are the local trains. Most foreign businessmen don't have much to do with those either, though they're a way to meet the real people if you have time to kill. Unfortunately, the line which runs from Guangzhou almost halfway to Gaozhou is a local line, which means I've ridden a local passenger train that consisted entirely of box cars. Each car had an iron grille across the door and an attendant who let down a ladder when the train pulled into a station. The attendant also had a torch which he shone on the ceiling in the tunnels. It was a slow, quiet ride, but I descended the ladder wet and dirty from the steam and soot blowing into the car from the steam engine.

For most Chinese the bulk of business travel is on the inter-mediate class of service which is diesel-powered or, on steep gradients, even electrified. For long journeys there are four classes of service: standing, seated, lying and deluxe. Foreign General Managers are encouraged to stick to deluxe. The cars are imported from East Germany (some fairly recently). They're air-conditioned and comfortable, with quiet, four-person com-partments. The attendants keep them clean, serve passengers tea in chinaware cups and provide slippers. If they've been careful about boiling the drinking water it can be a pleasant journey. It costs about as much as travelling the same distance by air.

Chinese employees, even joint-venture employees, normally don't travel in deluxe class; it's one of the perks reserved for cadres. Others can use it, but they must pay in Foreign Exchange Certificates. You might think this would ensure a better class of people, and from the Chinese perspective it does. Cadres are, by definition, a better class. But that doesn't mean they don't smoke, spit and throw their rubbish on the carpet.

Most trains have a carriage of deluxe compartments and, with the class exclusion, this carriage usually has berths available. Nevertheless, I sometimes find myself travelling in ordinary 'hard bed' class. Except in the hottest or coldest weather this is no real hardship. A hard-bed car contains about 100 bunks in racks three high. It's a bit dark and dingy, always crowded, and the floor quickly gets messy with rubbish. If you have a good relationship with the unit buying the tickets they'll do whatever is necessary to get you a middle bunk. People sit on the lower bunks all day, and the top bunks have low headroom and no view out the windows. At one end of the car is a squat toilet and at the other a Western-style appliance. The squat is usually prefer-able, but neither is very nice. I find hard-bed travel enjoyable enough, provided I remember to bring my own toilet paper and don't drink the water.

About half the carriages on most trains are of this hard-bed type; the rest are seat coaches. The seats start out reserved at the originating station, but after that it's every man for himself. At each station there's a mad dash when the waiting-room gate is opened. Travellers scramble to get to the seats of those who have just alighted, though there are usually plenty of standees who immediately grab any seat that becomes available. So most of the platform dashers are doomed to join the standees and sit on their baggage until someone with a seat gets off at a later station.

Chinese trains can be a relaxing and enjoyable way to travel, and the tickets are cheap. Getting the tickets is the tricky bit. Every station has long and fairly unruly queues at the ticket windows. Even at small rural stations this is the norm, because in a station with little business the ticket seller opens the window for only a few minutes before each train. So buying a ticket at the station is invariably a difficult business.

The easy way is simply to send someone else to do the dirty work. But the real secret of success is always to take a train originating at that station. In a little office far from the ticket windows, perhaps not even in the station building, a functionary allocates seats on the trains that will originate in that town during the coming week. A work unit with a relationship can send a representative there up to a week in advance to reserve a place. The ticket will be prepared, and the representative has only to return a few days later to pick it up. About three days before the train leaves, any leftover tickets go on general sale. These are the ones people fight over in the queues or buy from scalpers. By the time general sale opens the best seats are already gone.

Every work unit maintains some sort of relationship with the local station, just as Gold Land does with the Gaozhou bus station. When I'm going on a trip I usually already have a relationship with a local work unit in the destination city, so I get them to buy the return tickets. They're glad to do it, as they can use Gold Land's money to strengthen their own relationship with the station. As a foreigner I can always appeal to the China International Travel Service if there's an office in the town. If the town is too small to have an office, it's likely to be small enough that just showing a foreign face in the right office at the station will do the trick.

One aspect of the class system is that different individuals are expected to pay different fares for the same service. Train fares for foreign tourists are double or triple the basic fare for ordinary Chinese. When buying plane or train tickets, travellers have to show their identification papers and are charged accordingly. Our Hong Kong visitors and foreign customers pay the top price, but local employees can do better. As Gold Land's General Manager I can legitimately claim the domestic price and pay in Chinese currency rather than in Foreign Exchange Certificates. Just because I'm entitled to it doesn't mean I always succeed, but to have any hope of success I always carry a temporary residence permit (rather than a passport) and a letter over the stamp of the Gaozhou Foundry (rather than Gold Land) explaining that I'm managing the work unit and travelling on company business. I also carry some cash or cigarettes. These letters are also useful with hotels, the police and in various other situations. If I still have no success I can only console myself that the amount involved isn't worth fighting over. Foreign aid workers and teachers are issued a form known as a 'white card' which helps them to pay in local currency rather than in Foreign Exchange Certificates, but a joint venture's employees have to argue their way through without the card.

Every railroad station maintains a special waiting-room for deluxe passengers. In large stations these rooms are heated and air-conditioned, and have tea laid on. An attendant informs the passengers if the train will be late and personally escorts them to the correct platform when it arrives. In small towns, deluxe passengers have to make do with the station manager's office and forgo the aircon, but they still get to avoid the stampede from the waiting-room gate.

If you find yourself travelling by boat or by bus you can forget about all of these distinctions of class, fare and accommodation.

On the bus it's every man for himself. Chinese buses usually come complete with vomit stains trailing from the windows, which should serve as a warning that they're for special situations only. Nevertheless, certain major cities such as Hefei, the capital of Anhui Province, are best reached by bus if you have no car. If you ask around there will often be a single night run which uses an air-conditioned bus of Polish or Czech manufacture. It will cost about 50 per cent more than the regular fare, but it might have reasonably comfortable seats and no standees. Some even have videos, though this isn't necessarily a positive feature. Normally, though, my contacts would never let me leave town on a bus. Visitors to Gold Land never hesitate to ask us to send one of our vehicles 500 km to pick them up and save them the bus trip.

China's boat network is extensive. The boats are slower even than the buses, but they tend to be scheduled for overnight runs, so this needn't be a drawback. Unlike the bus they're quiet and cool, so you can get a good night's sleep. The interior is usually laid out in the form of long shelves divided into bunks by low wooden dividers. There's no privacy; you sleep in your clothes. But they have reliable power and often refrigerators, so it's pleasant to sit by the window with a cold beer. You probably wouldn't want to eat or drink anything else sold on board. They may not take their water from the river, but it wouldn't be wise to count on it. As with the buses, tickets are available only at the pier or on the boat, but we have a contact at the port nearest to Gaozhou who uses his relationship at the boat company to get us a breezy spot in a forward compartment away from the engine. Again, I always try to embark at the originating port to have a choice of berths.

After all that preamble, it shouldn't be surprising that the first rule of all this plane, train and other travel is to avoid it. Foreigners, export customers, general managers and even ordinary joint-venture managers don't ride this kind of public transport except in unusual circumstances. If the destination is less than four days away it is in every way preferable for us to appear in the splendour of our best truck, with the Gold Land logo painted on the door.

In most factories the choice of vehicles is pretty limited, and for many years the best that the Gaozhou Foundry could claim was a white Japanese-made van. These days, Gold Land uses a Toyota sedan. The attitude towards these vehicles is in many ways a flashback to the 1930s in the West. Joe Lee, the Shipping Manager, is nominally in charge of our fleet; but in fact fleet management is an unofficial, but major, preoccupation of Mr Chow, the Chairman of the Board. It would be fair to say that it's a rare day when our Chairman doesn't make at least one decision concerning who should use which vehicle for which purpose, since there is no clearer and more decisive indicator of status than who is allocated which vehicle in a given situation. The sedan, in particular, is Mr Chow's personal preserve. He is rarely seen using one of the other vehicles, and lends 'his' car to others only as a mark of favour. In fact, the sedan is one of the cheaper vehicles to run; but when allocating vehicles, cost is relatively unimportant in light of status considerations. In a quiet, air-conditioned vehicle, travel-as-a-perk really comes into its own, so when there's a junket in prospect there is always a long list of eager candidates for any extra places.

Since I'm more widely travelled than my Chinese colleagues it falls to me to arrange provisioning for the trip. From departure to destination our van-capsule will be cut off from our network of friends and contacts, so it behoves us to be self-sufficient. It's virtually impossible, for example, to stop for a cup of tea on the way. There are many roadside restaurants of various standards, but none that cater for a quick pot of tea and a piece of cake. Things go better, then, if I can remember to ask someone to lay in a supply of biscuits and individual bottles of mineral water for the journey.

Cars are rare in most parts of China, but that doesn't mean the traffic is light. For hour after hour our car is the fastest vehicle on a highway teeming with pedestrians, ox-carts, cyclists, garden tractors and old and decrepit Chinese trucks. It makes for difficult and dangerous driving.

In most parts of China a van is easily the most prestigious and comfortable vehicle on the road. The driver feels to some extent that the van (and he) should be the centre of attention as he graces passing roadside villages. He would not entirely dismiss the suggestion that other road-users should make way and defer to him. Driving at night gives evidence of this attitude. Many drivers will dip their headlights for on-coming cars and trucks, but not for motorcycles. And when faced with tractors, cyclists or pedestrians, many drivers immediately switch to high beam.

Although a car-load of my Gold Land colleagues have schemed to secure a place on the trip, the novelty soon palls. None of them is accustomed to travelling on anything more substantial than a bicycle, and after a few minutes most begin to feel twinges of motion sickness. The best antidote is sleep, and my colleagues doze most of the time, even on a multi-day trip.

My companions' interest in the journey, despite their malaise, quickly focuses on the meals. Since they are travelling with me, they're not obliged to contribute to the meals from their *per diem*, so there is invariably strong pressure to seek out the best establishment in town for each meal stop. This is just as well.

It's not that the food is any better in these places. At least in Guangdong Province, the standard of cuisine is uniformly high and the food is invariably tasty wherever we might choose to stop. The matting-and-bamboo shacks by the road are, if anything, probably cleaner than the big hotel dining rooms. These little joints have no pretensions, and bring all the dishes and chopsticks to the table in a basin of boiling water. I have sometimes been told that I'm the first foreigner ever to visit. It certainly seems plausible, as they often bring out brand-new chopsticks for me, still wrapped and sealed from the (probably unsanitary) factory. No, the problem with the roadside joints is neither quality not sanitation. It's more a matter of ambiance.

I once hosted a group of high-ranking party and government officials from Gaozhou on their first visit to Hong Kong, and we dined at a distinguished Western restaurant. It could have been a blunder, but fortunately the waiter was up to the occasion. He very discreetly and politely made it clear to my distinguished guests that they should use the ashtrays for their cigarettes, neither spit nor throw their fish-bones on the carpet and generally do their best to imitate the manners of the diners at the other tables. Many Western tourists in Hong Kong are appalled by the standard of restaurant decorum. China, I'm afraid, operates much further from Western norms. In many ways, it's often difficult to stomach the delicious food if your eyes should wander from your bowl to what's going on around you. So, when travelling, I give full rein to my colleagues' champagne tastes. They're at least likely to lead me to an establishment where the spittoons are emptied.

In the vagaries of travel, things won't always work out this way; and from time to time the party finds itself patronising a roadside private restaurant. Overlook the ambiance, for there is no other solution. Relax, and think of sociology. Or rather, think of prostitution. Everyone else is.

For many years prostitution has been strongly suppressed in China, and venereal disease has been much reduced. With the return of private enterprise, entrepreneurs are opening small roadhouse restaurants outside the towns. Since they depend on the local market for all their supplies, the competitors on any one stretch of highway inevitably end up offering much the same dishes, service and prices. It doesn't take years at business school to teach them niche marketing.

To think of these young country waitresses as prostitutes in the Western sense does them something of an injustice. I think of them instead as a very rudimentary sort of geisha. Each restaurant has only one or two. Between mealtimes, when the restaurant is empty, they sit at the outer edge of the parking area smiling and waving at the drivers of passing vehicles. If a customer stops in while the place isn't busy, they'll sit at his table and enjoy a glass of beer and some conversation. And if he should fancy a little something after dinner . . . I speculate that like many products and services in China, this one is basic, but fair enough value at the price. In 1989 the going rate was only about 2 yuan in these roadside eateries, 20 in a small city hotel and up to 200 in the tourist hotels of the major cities. Even at those prices, however, indulging in 'dessert' wouldn't be a good idea for a foreign manager. The whole business would immediately be public knowledge around the factory.

Travel in China need not be a hassle or particularly expensive. For a work unit manager it can be rather like a royal progress with himself as the king. He has only to observe a few simple rules: always rely on his network for hospitality; don't rely on his staff to plan the trip; and try not to eat too much at the banquets. Then sit back and watch the countryside roll slowly by the window. In China I relish every opportunity to travel on business.

10

In protective custody

W HATEVER the difficulties of running a factory in China, it's not bandit country. The laws are clear. The police, the militia and the army are everywhere, and they do their duty. Foreign investors who manage to uphold their side of a joint-venture agreement can be fairly confident that the Chinese will do their best to uphold the other side. It's true that extenuating circumstances arise rather more often than in more developed countries, but the Chinese are accustomed to problems of that sort. That's why in any negotiation they emphasise the need for goodwill and a spirit of co-operation.

Why is it then that so many of these joint-venture relationships seem to end in tears? I suspect this may be more apparent than real, as the problem cases get all the publicity while the successful ventures roll quietly along. Certainly there are thousands of joint ventures which have been negotiated and even signed, but which have never managed to get into operation. For the Chinese partner, this is undoubtedly a big disappointment—the chance of a lifetime missed—and probably a smaller disap pointment to the foreign partner as well. But the real disasters—where the hotel has been built but the local government won't issue a business licence—are a well-publicised few.

Everything grinds to a halt because the spirit of co-operation evaporates and the relationships go sour. It has never been alleged that joint ventures are made in heaven. It requires plenty of goodwill and understanding to make them work, and even then they sometimes fail. But it won't be because men with machine-guns seize the cash box, or men in Mao jackets seize the bank account.

In a lawless society lawlessness doesn't cause much of a stir, while in a law-abiding society every little incident makes the headlines. By this measure China is confirmed as a pretty law-abiding place. If a Chinese driver can't park his vehicle in a guarded car-park he will leave someone behind to watch it. A Chinese buying a packet of cigarettes will often open the packet and smoke one in the shop on suspicion that he may have been sold an inferior brand in a counterfeit package. Some Hong Kong residents fear that if they visit China they'll be drugged and butchered by thugs anxious to sell their eyes and kidneys. I don't lose any sleep over it. My foreign kidneys probably wouldn't fit. On the contrary, I figure that if the Chinese get excited about such petty crime and ghost stories it must be a pretty safe society.

Most foreigners find that their life of crime in China centres around the Customs regulations and foreign exchange controls. A joint venture is not supposed to have any trouble on either of these scores. It's supposed to be able to arrange duty-free import of all necessary equipment and supplies and to sell its foreign exchange revenue on a special auction market offering international rates. In fact, both of these systems work quite well as far as they go. The problems arise when the office runs out of white corrector fluid, or you need 5 yuan in local currency to get your hair cut. These are the situations where bureaucracy will drive you to a life of crime.

China's import regulations are not much different from those of any developing country. They are meant to prevent travellers bringing in sought-after foreign radios, refrigerators and motorcycles and selling them in the local market to the detriment of the local manufacturers of undesirable non-working models. On entering the country, visitors must fill out a declaration listing anything they are carrying which might be saleable, and on the way out the Customs are meant to verify that they still have it all with them. The system catches cameras and wrist-watches, and if I brought in a dozen bottles of corrector fluid still packed

167

together in the original case I might have some trouble there, too. But the Customs officials usually can't read foreign languages, so if I spread the bottles around through my luggage they probably assume it's some sort of medicine. Most joint ventures bring in a wide variety of their supplies in this way and no harm is done.

Major equipment is a more difficult problem. It calls for careful planning at the time of the initial joint-venture agreement. Items mentioned in the agreement—even computers, vehicles or production equipment—can be brought in duty free for business use. The foreign staff can also specify personal belongings, again including a car, that they will bring in with them duty free. But it's difficult to change your mind and add things later. In principle, the partners would have to negotiate a new agreement. This is such a problem that it's usually these after-thoughts that lead joint-venture employees into a life of crime.

The modern Western technology we've introduced at Gold Land includes a photocopier and a fax machine. In each case, we bought portable models. We have two of each and leave one in Hong Kong. When something needs maintenance we ask our next visitor to bring in the second unit and declare it on his Customs form. On leaving, he can leave the working unit with us and take back the other to satisfy the Customs inspector. Then we get it serviced in Hong Kong. It's not strictly legal, but again no harm is done.

Currency controls are quite another matter. In theory, China's yuan is not convertible, and only souvenir quantities can be taken out of the country. Foreigners working in China can be paid in yuan; in which case they have no shortage of haircut money, as they're obliged by law to spend at least half their income in the country. (Or, more precisely, they can legally change only half of what they have received into foreign currencies to be taken out when they leave.) Foreigners don't like this option, as there are simply not enough things worth buying. The alternative is to be paid abroad and to purchase small amounts of local currency for daily use. However, doing it this way, they don't receive yuan in exchange. They're given instead Foreign Exchange Certificates, which is a sort of special convertible currency for foreigners.

This works well enough in the big cities where banks keep the special certificates in stock and where most businesses will accept them in payment, but in Gaozhou it's hopeless. When I want to buy certificates the bank doesn't have them, and when I want a haircut the barber wants real money.

The solution is the black market. There is a black market in foreign currency, and even in the Foreign Exchange Certificates, because both are useful to ordinary citizens in certain special circumstances. In particular, anyone hoping to travel abroad has to begin accumulating foreign exchange and/or the certificates well in advance. The market is made by a shady lot of illegal money changers who lurk in big city locations frequented by foreigners. Every once in a while the police round up a bunch and shoot them.

If they catch a foreigner dealing on the black market he won't be shot, but he might well be expelled. And in any case, collective responsibility sticks to his work unit. So I'm obliged to proceed very carefully. In fact, I'm never short of trusted contacts who feel for one reason or another that they would like to accumulate some foreign currency. Since Gold Land is generating exports we're entitled to a certain number of exit visas every year for foreign travel. Anyone eligible for one of those trips must be interested in purchasing foreign cash. In the paltry amounts I need for personal expenses we're not likely to have any trouble.

Which is not to say that no one will find out. The neighbourhood committee keeps an eye on the social relations of the citizens of each neighbourhood, and we have a similar set-up within our factory housing. They don't for the most part extend their many services to the General Manager's quarters, but the little old 'Madame Defarges' who sit around in the courtyard all day watching everyone's comings and goings have been asked to keep a special eye on the foreigner. While this makes my quarters burglar-proof despite the likely presence of a walkman, camera and other sought-after consumer goods, certain visitors might be asked for their identity papers and a brief explanation. Not normally, you understand, but anyone who stays overnight, for example.

My quarters are actually part of the factory guesthouse, which is managed by a housekeeper. This is certainly convenient, especially when it comes to shopping and preparing meals. I behave myself, so nothing has occurred to highlight the fact that the housekeeper has been asked to keep an eye on me. On the other hand, during my first few weeks in Gaozhou I discovered that this housekeeper had a son who wanted to tag along whenever I proposed going for a run or a bicycle ride into the surrounding countryside.

A Don Juan with a fatal attraction for the local girls would no doubt find these arrangements distinctly inconvenient, but for most of us it works quite the other way around. Whatever a foreigner's conduct, however innocent, his every move is a rich new resource for the work unit's gossip mill. A little factual input from a minder probably helps to keep the wilder attributions under control.

This protective custody doesn't, as you might suppose, smother the joint venture. We get along quite well in the present situation. But what's the probability that the whole edifice will come crashing down? And if it did, what would happen to our investment? What's the political risk, as they say?

I'm not going to pretend that I can answer these questions. In the end, we each have to make our own judgements. But when the system changed in Hungary and Poland, Western firms which had been operating under the communist system weren't swept away in the transition. Indeed, they found that they had a head start. It's my opinion that the demise of Communism in China will come quietly, and that it will affect primarily the politicos in Beijing, as the mass of the population is basically apathetic and compliant. This apathy was amply demonstrated at the time of the Tiananmen Square massacre in 1989.

History will perhaps record May 1989 as a turning point in Chinese history; a time of dramatic events of world-wide significance. But in Gaozhou it was a bit of a non-event. At the beginning of the month one of the local preoccupations was gang rivalry among secondary-school students. Students at some of the local middle schools had formed gangs with macho names, and in the evenings these groups were organising small 'rumbles' in the manner of *West Side Story*. The facts were probably rather tame, but in the imaginations of the citizens all sorts of violence and evil were possible. The streets were rumoured to be unsafe in the evening. Our factory even organised a little defence squad to spring into action in the unlikely event that these young boys should find a cast iron foundry a tempting target for their depredations. So as the great events began to unfold in Beijing, Gold Land at least could claim to be prepared for the worst.

Almost everyone I spoke to at the time sympathised with the students' demands for less corruption in government. The pervasive 'relationships' ensure that every ordinary Chinese citizen has personal experience of official corruption and abuse of power. At the same time, they all expressed respect for the Chinese nation, the 1949 revolution, socialism and even the Communist Party. It's important to remember that the student revolutionaries were not challenging the principles of Marxism or even of Leninism. Their complaints were much more specifically targeted at individuals who exploited their government and party positions for personal gain. When the students spoke of freedom and democracy, they perhaps understood that they were challenging Leninist doctrine. But the people in general were not making this distinction. They simply hoped for a more egalitarian style of leadership which would mitigate some of the exploitation routinely practised by those holding government or party power.

I never heard of anyone out in the countryside who contemplated demonstrating in support of the students. Throughout Chinese history the residents of the country areas have been essentially feudal vassals of one or another central authority. They calmly accept the idea that decisions are made at the centre and in due course will be communicated to them; they have only to follow the official line. The idea of contributing to decision making by, for example, demonstrating does not easily occur to them. University students have this revolutionary tradition, but the students are future cadres. They are a tiny minority of the population and definitely a class apart from the residents of a country town.

As it happens, a group of local secondary-school students visited me during the period of the Beijing demonstrations. 'What are you guys doing here?' I chided. 'How come you're sitting in my office when you're supposed to be out demonstrating?' As usual, they mistook my sarcasm for serious criticism.

'But we're only middle-school students,' they protested. 'It's university and technical-college students who are demonstrating, not middle-school students.'

If Gaozhou had had a local university the students might have been expected to demonstrate in solidarity with their Beijing comrades. And the local workers might well have joined the demonstration as their worker comrades in Beijing had done. But with no student group to lead the way the workers seemed incapable of taking the lead locally, since that is not how it was being done in Beijing. And, of course, most of the local workers are not 'workers' at all but peasants who, instead of working on the farm, happen to be working in a shop or factory in the town. The radio reports made no mention of peasant participation in the events in Beijing. Without this lead from the centre it was unlikely that the local peasants would think to take a lead in policy making, whatever their individual or collective dissatisfaction with the old order.

This is not to say that there was no interest in the students' activities. On the contrary, they provided matchless entertainment. Chinese radio and television are not normally very entertaining. And candid reporting of events embarrassing to the government was a definite novelty. But during the early days of the protest, until the departure of President Gorbachev, the television and radio reported fully on developments; and their reporting agreed for the most part with the facts reported on the Voice of America and BBC World Service. From May 20th, with the declaration of martial law, foreign journalists' reports were restricted and the Chinese media reverted to their usual government-controlled coverage. Until then we had been seeing ample live coverage from Tiananmen Square, some of it apparently supplied by Western TV networks. The unusual candour had people glued to their radios and TVs (or at least to those of their neighbours), and the latest developments were a constant topic of conversation in the factory.

For me, the most dramatic moment of the whole affair was a

very peaceful moment indeed. On Thursday, May 18th, the full moon shone from a clear sky. It was the first really hot day of summer, and all afternoon and into the evening we had experienced a complete power cut. As there were no lights or fans, many of the managers assembled during the evening on the roof of the office building to catch a little cool night air. On that day the unrest had spread to a small city about 50 km away where there is a minor teacher-training college. We sat in the dark on the roof and listened to the local radio station broadcasting live on-the-spot reports of the relatively small and peaceful demonstration almost at our doorstep. Then someone arrived from town to report that the police were lining the streets on the excuse that they anticipated trouble from the gangs of secondary-school students who might exploit the national unrest to break a few windows on the main street. In the end, even this never developed, but power to our part of town had been cut off to increase the minimal street lighting in the main street. It gave us a feeling of being in touch with the great events.

On May 22nd, five weeks after the start of the disturbances, official reaction finally made it to our part of the country. Mr Chin, our Party Secretary, was called to a meeting at the local party headquarters, and on the 23rd he convened a meeting of all the managers and the main party members in the factory to transmit the results.

He began by reading Li Peng's speech invoking martial law, then continued with some embellishments which might have been his own, but more probably came from the party meeting. The most interesting was an assertion that the whole thing had been fomented by the United States. None of his listeners took that charge very seriously, and when I later asked him how he could make such a patently unreasonable allegation he replied only that he had 'heard people say it'. Managers were reminded to 'defend social order' and report anyone not turning up for work. If the truant proved to have been absent for purposes of demonstrating, the managers should apply some ideological re-education. The managers were also asked to refrain from spreading rumours. The definition of a rumour was clarified by the further suggestion that if managers had any opinions they should report them to the leaders rather than discuss them with the other employees. Finally, after all of this damage control, his last point was about corruption: 'Don't tolerate corruption; report it to your leaders or to the police.' An interesting point to find at the bottom of his agenda, as this was the demonstrating students' main complaint.

I had been working in the factory for about a year at that time, and this was the first time we had called a meeting of this kind. I had read, of course, that during the Cultural Revolution these meetings were the main daily activity. And I was aware that the party network of the old work unit had been maintained intact in the new joint-venture company. But this was the first time it had been called into action in at least a year. It was easy to imagine how this process had imposed thought and behaviour control so effectively and, though a bit rusty, there was no doubt that it could do so again. Everyone realised it, and listened deferentially throughout.

On June 1st the party in Beijing published a 'Restoration of Order' document which finally reached us and was read in another meeting on June 5th. This was the document that actually announced the fall of Zhao Ziyang, though weeks later I was still hearing 'rumours' of its existence on the foreign shortwave radio stations. The document purported to include an extract from the minutes of a meeting of party leaders held on May 22nd at which a whole series of the survivors took the opportunity to declare their dedication to Leninism, to list the various 'mistakes' of Zhao and to warn everyone that patience has its limits. It was lucky timing, really. The document was written at the time of the phoney war, when the troops sent in to break up the demonstrations had been stopped by masses of civilians. But the document arrived in Gaozhou just after the massacre and it put the best possible gloss on what everyone agreed were pretty inexcusable events. It showed the party as decisive, in control, but staying its hand in the face of provocation.

A good try, but arriving as it did right after the massacre it got little respect. Even our most loyal party members complained to me privately that they were disgusted and (at that point) thought that Zhao had gotten a raw deal. Even our Mr Chin didn't dare to make the usual personal commentary on this document. Instead, he asked Mr So to read it through twice, then everyone went back to work. Mr Chin didn't want to tempt anyone into saying something that he might later be called upon to punish. And at the same time he couldn't be entirely sure himself that the massacre would end the story. In Guangdong, at least, people knew of the massacre; disgust was universal and there seemed a distinct possibility that this time the government had carried Leninism too far.

It was a close-run affair. During the week after the massacre one of the world's most successful thought-control systems was pulled out of mothballs, dusted off and put into action. The basis of it all was the 'Big Lie' that it was soldiers, not students, who had been killed in Tiananmen Square. Basically, the citizens knew this wasn't true. But the carefully edited television clips which repeated over and over scenes of violence against soldiers slowly defused the utter outrage against the army and the régime. On June 6th Mr Chin got new marching orders as the provincial, regional and county party organisations fell into line. These were read to the factory managers and party members on June 9th and got down to such admonitions as no wearing black armbands, talk to your children about the Cultural Revolution, no panic buying and no 'spreading rumours'. Party members were told to follow the party line or their memberships would be cancelled. By June 15th, outrage had gradually mellowed into smouldering discontent.

Since June 1989 the government has done what it can to rebuild its position. In particular, there have been well-publicised and reasonably vigorous campaigns to stamp out corruption and the abuse of power. If you're tempted to imagine that these campaigns have been successful, better go back to Chapter 1 and start again. In China, 'relationships' are the essence of Communism. If one hand refused to wash the other, nothing would ever get done.

So far, the effects of the 1989 protests have been largely negative: the leadership was frightened out of participating in the reforms that have swept the rest of the Communist world. Once again, China has turned in on itself and been left behind. Let's hope it won't last long. The people deserve better.

175

Index